Nightclub Womenz

by

Patrick Scott Barnes

All rights reserved. Unless using for articles or reviews, no part of this book may be used without permission from the author/photographer.

ISBN: 9798672847894

Copyright © 2020 Patrick Scott Barnes

This book is dedicated to Shana MacDonald, Tony Mims, and Colin Spencer.

Facebook page: Patrick Scott Barnes
Website: Patrickscottbarnes.com
Instagram: stonecrazy89
Email: Patrickbarne@gmail.com

Copies available on Amazon.com.

Table of Contents

Introduction..Page 5

Poems

A Social Media Lie..Page 9
Booze in One Hand, Camera in the Other..Page 12
Spider-Man's Racial Identity..Page 16
Standing Out..Page 20
English Teacher..Page 24
Losing the House...Page 28
Judging Women...Page 32
Nocturnal Creature..Page 36
Fighting Love Addiction..Page 40
Take It Down, Please...Page 44
An Adult Child's Mixed Emotions...Page 48

Introduction

As of this writing, the whole world is experiencing the Covid-19 pandemic. The same virus is tearing up my home state. Right now, when it comes to the coronavirus, Florida holds one of the highest death toll rates in the country.

During these scary times, I usually follow these three things. First, I drive to work. After work, wearing a mask, I stop by Wal-Mart. Then finally, I drive home.

I rarely go out. Folks with underlying health conditions are more likely to die from Covid-19. My underlying heath condition? High blood pressure. So, that's why I usually stay my ass home.

So, during this pandemic, what's a good way to pass time? I chose creating a photo book containing a few poems.

For two and a half years, I photographed a Downtown Orlando nightclub.

The first year, I photographed Fridays and Saturdays. On those nights, mostly hip-hop music played. The second year, my nights included Sundays. These nights contained mostly Tropical Latin music.

I always cared more about the women photos than I did the other pics. That's why I always uploaded the women photos to social media. I wanted my friends to see the beauties I encountered every weekend.

Because social media friends loved them, I placed some of those photos in this book. I included dancers, VIP bottle service women, bartenders, a future hip-hop star plus a woman dressed as a green M&M. Of course, I included the sexy patrons.

The nightclub isn't paying me to advertise for them. So, I'm not mentioning the place's name.

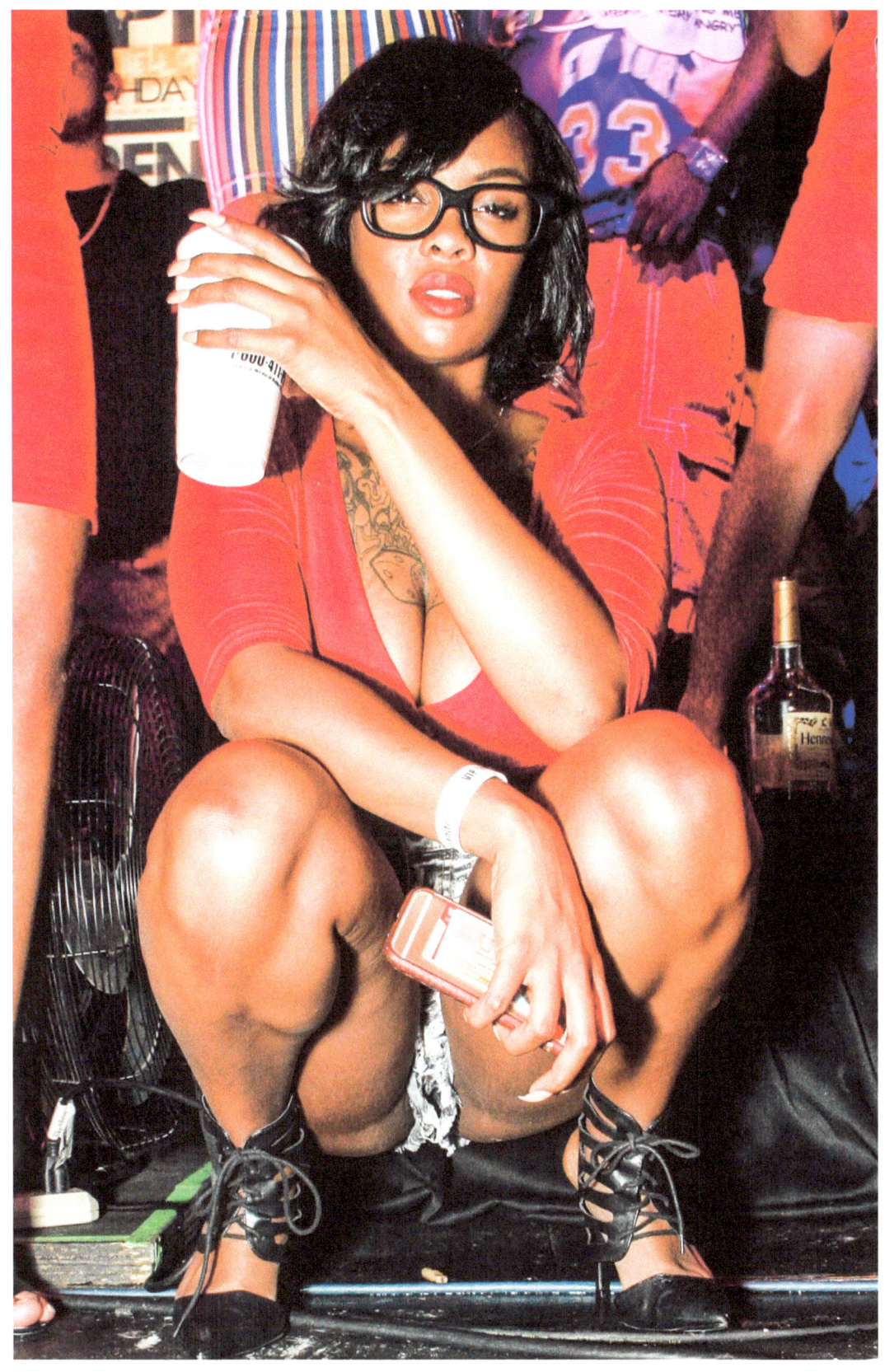

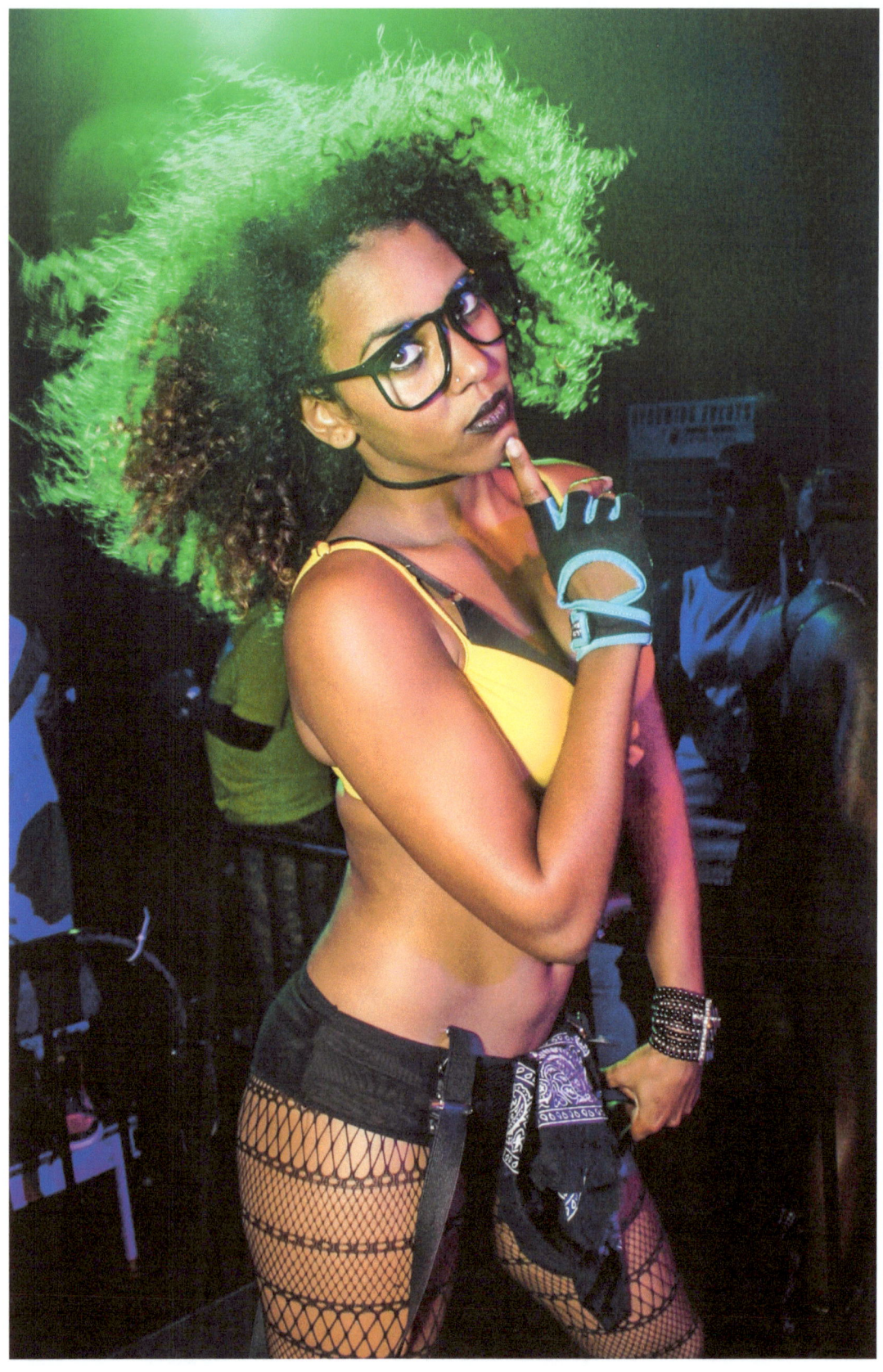

A Social Media Lie

Fooling social media.
Hiding behind a lie.
Uploading all the happy pics.
Happy selfies of me.
Happy selfies of relatives and me.
Happy selfies of friends and me.
Also, happy selfies with random women I'll never,
ever, see again.

Hiding behind a lie.
Hiding my depression.
Depression been dragging on for months.
Part of me still not over my mom's two-year death.
Still not over a broken romance.
One that wasn't good for me in the first place.
Knew this and dived in anyway.
Foreclosure coming soon.
Still don't have a place to move to.

Won't post these things on social media.
Still believing I must upload happy pics.
Or event pics.
Or beautiful scenery pics.
Or nightlife women pics.
Must keep that big lie going.
The big lie that says my life is so grand right now.

Is that true?
Must I keep that lie going?
Or is that all I in my head?
Don't know the answer.
Yet, I continue to fool social media.

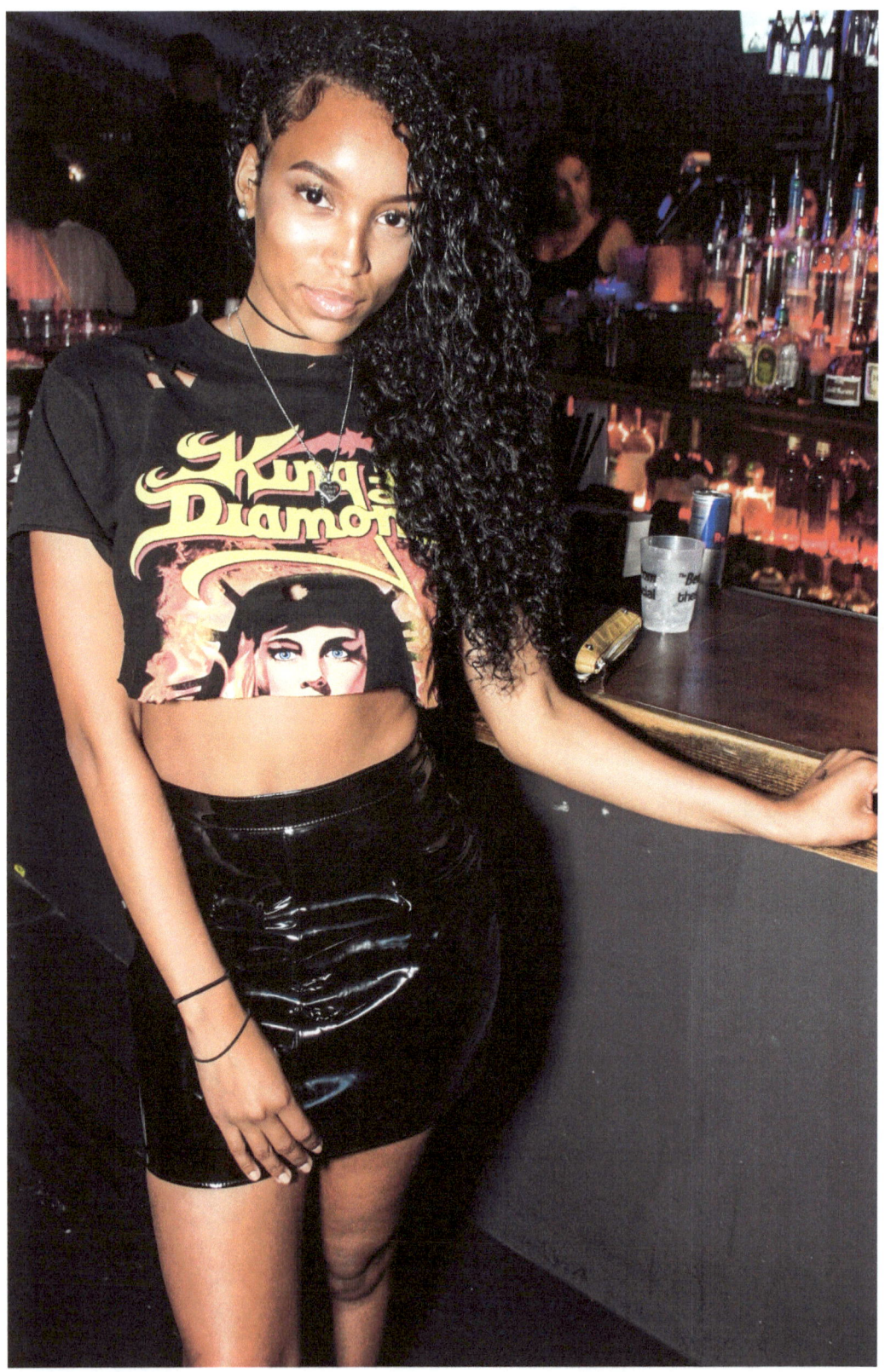

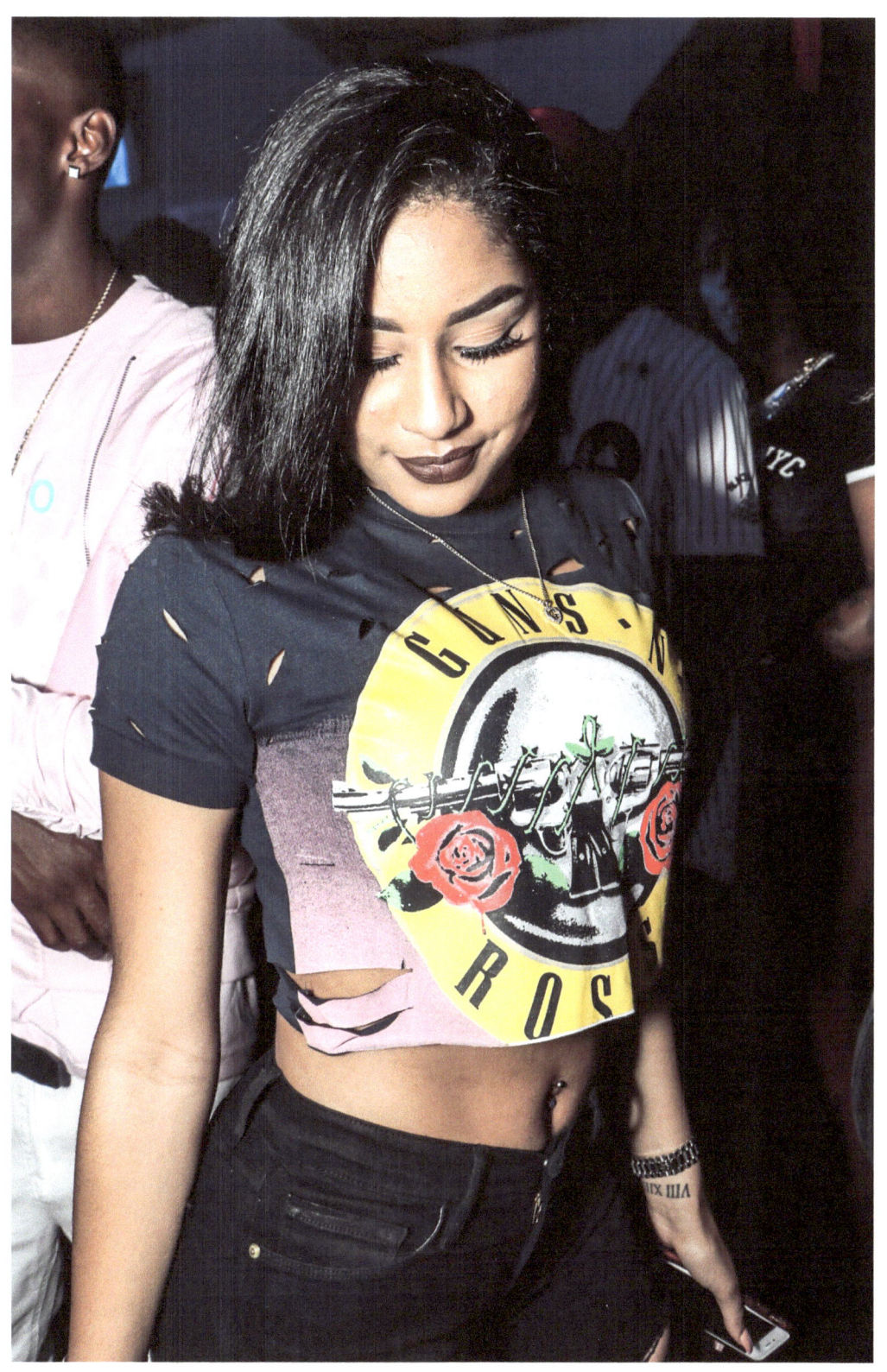

Booze in One Hand, Camera in the Other

Use to drink too much during nightclub photo gigs.
Some nights way worse than others.
Bud Light.
Cîroc.
(A white DJ turned me on to that "urban" drink.)
Long Island Iced Tea.
Sometimes two Long Island Iced Teas in one night.
Also, whatever else someone offered me.

Some nights not too bad.
Some nights outright booze fest.

Next morning arrives.
Nagging headache.
Seeing pics in my camera I don't remember taking.
Still don't remember taking them.

Surprised I never got into a fight.
Surprised I never got a DUI.
Surprised I never crashed into another car.

Guess I was just damned lucky.

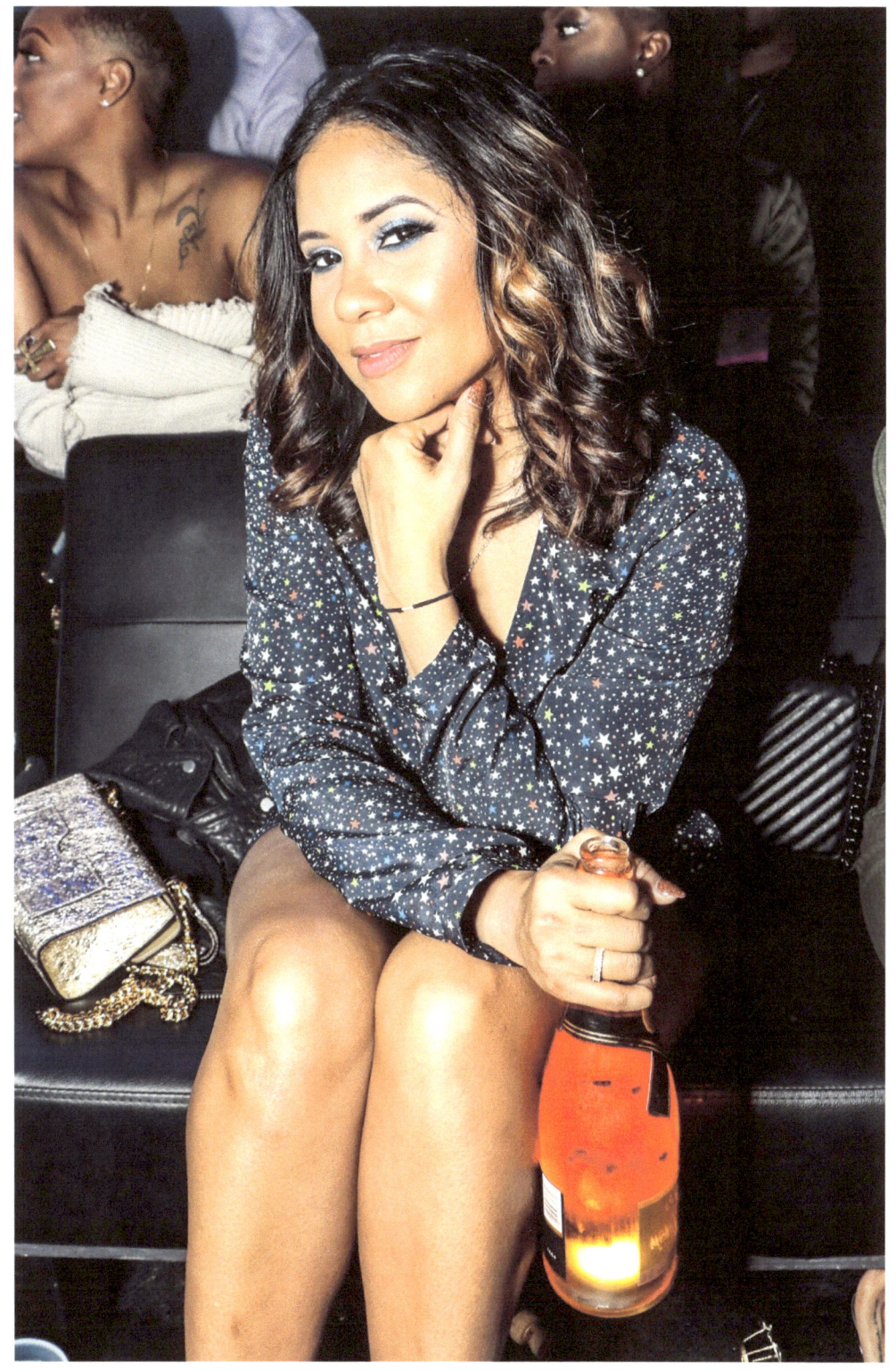

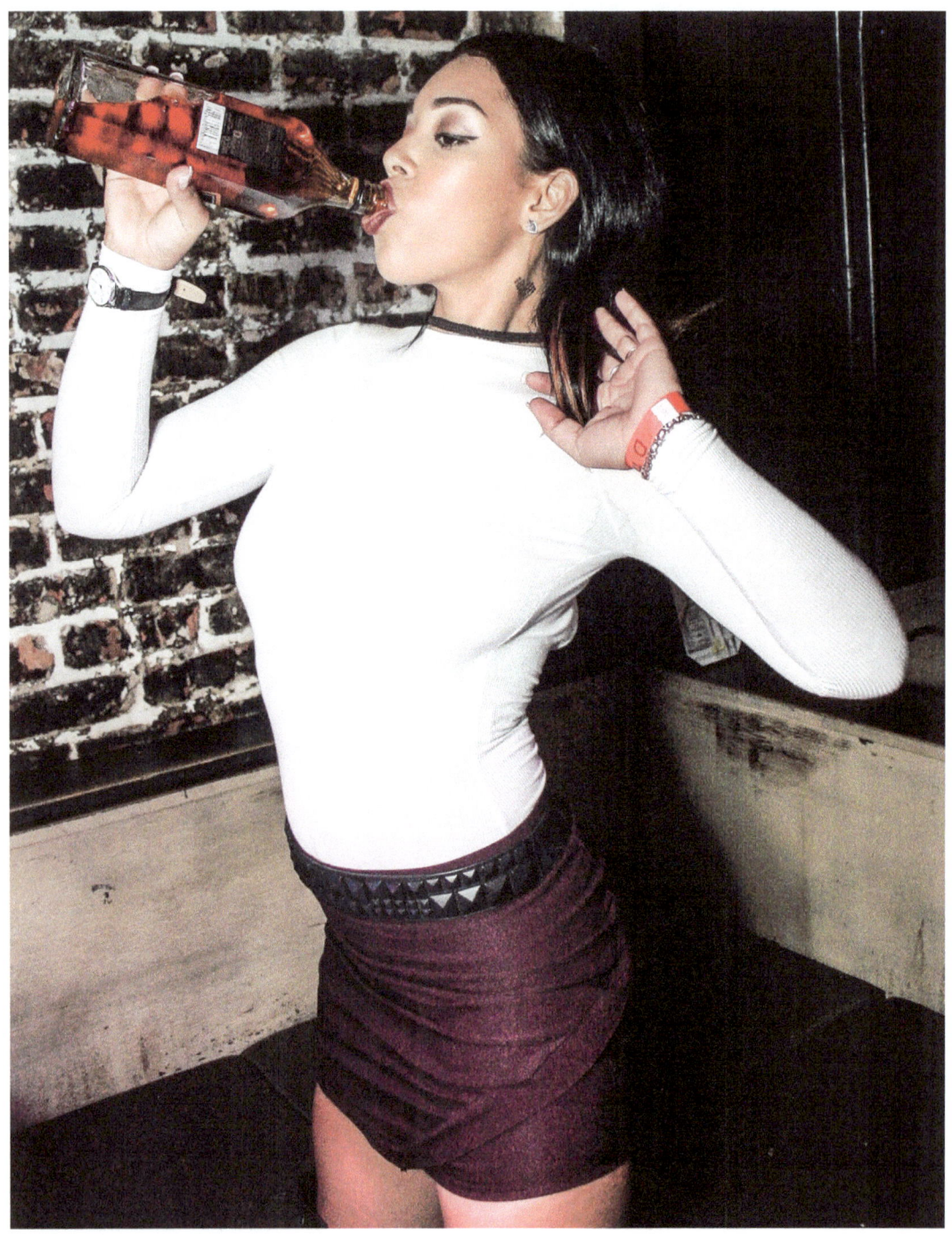

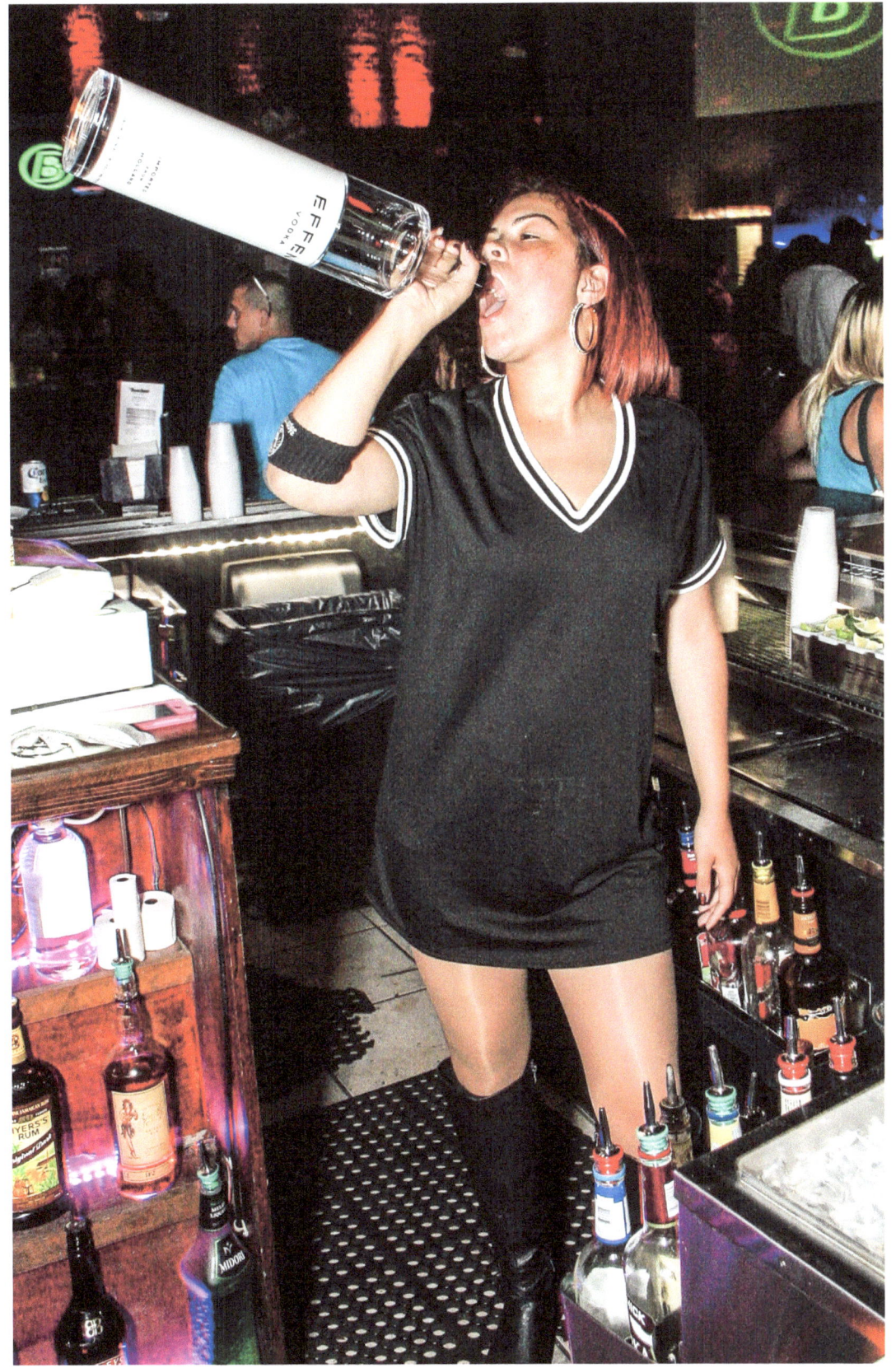

Spider-Man's Racial Identity

Second grade.
Forgot how it went.
Think it was during music class.
White classmate said he was Spider-Man.
Then, I said I was Spider-Man too.
Or something like that.
Classmate said Spider-Man wasn't black.

I do remember that part.

He pulled this before with another character.
Forgot which one.

Over thirty years pass.
Marvel Comics introduces Miles Morales.
A black Hispanic teenager.
In another universe, Miles fights crime as
Your Friendly Neighborhood Spider-Man.

Halloween season.
White friend tells social media his son wants to be Miles Morales.
Kid's mind was made up.
Says he's going to be Miles Morales for Halloween.

Finding this ironic.
White kid wants to be a black Hispanic superhero.
Remembering that classmate who told me
I couldn't be Spider-Man.
Why couldn't I be Spider-Man, you ask?
Because punk-ass Peter Parker wasn't black.

Have no problem with my friend's kid being Miles Morales.
Yet, as for that classmate of mine?
His kid or kids or grandkids can't be Black Panther.

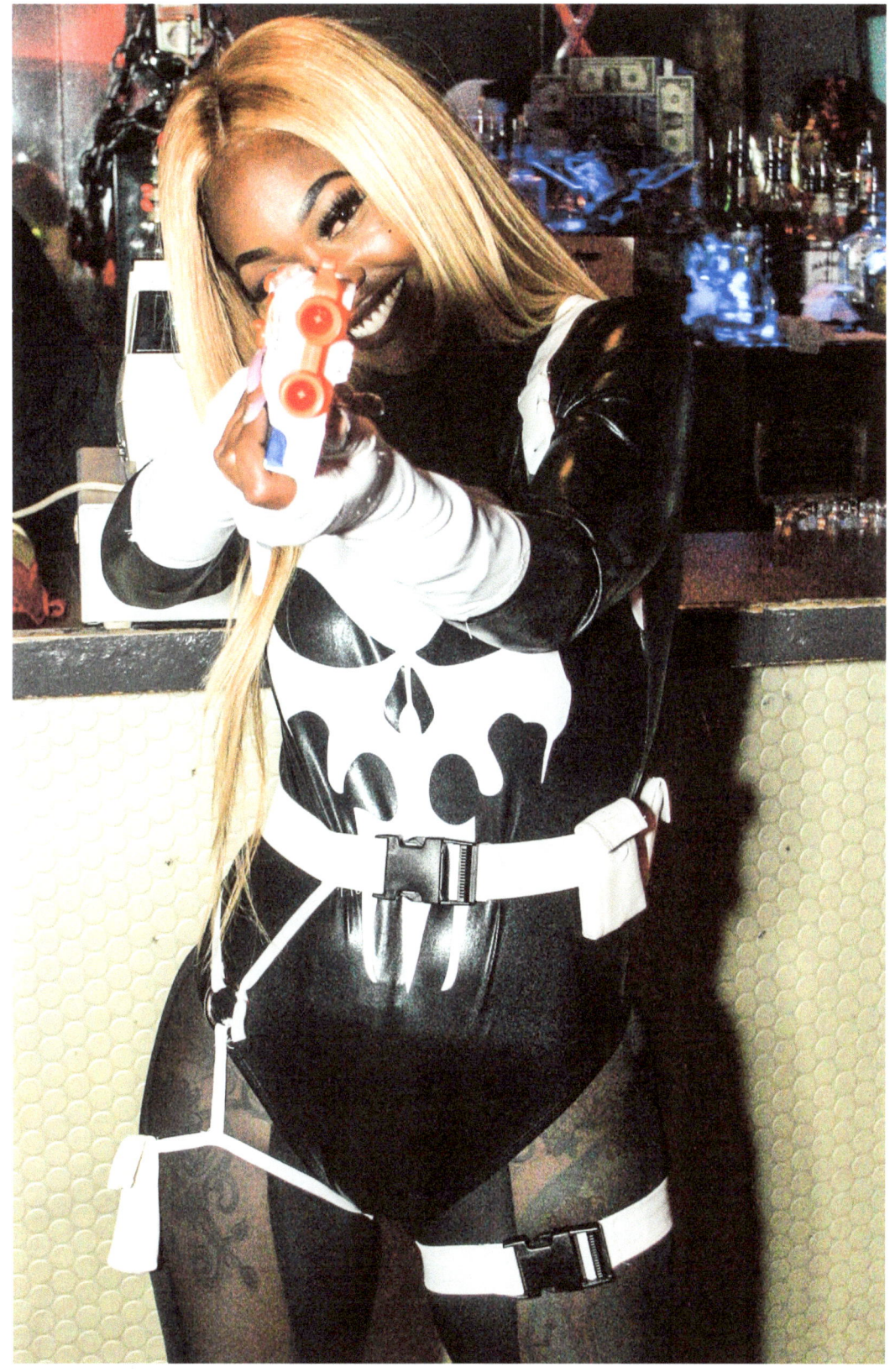

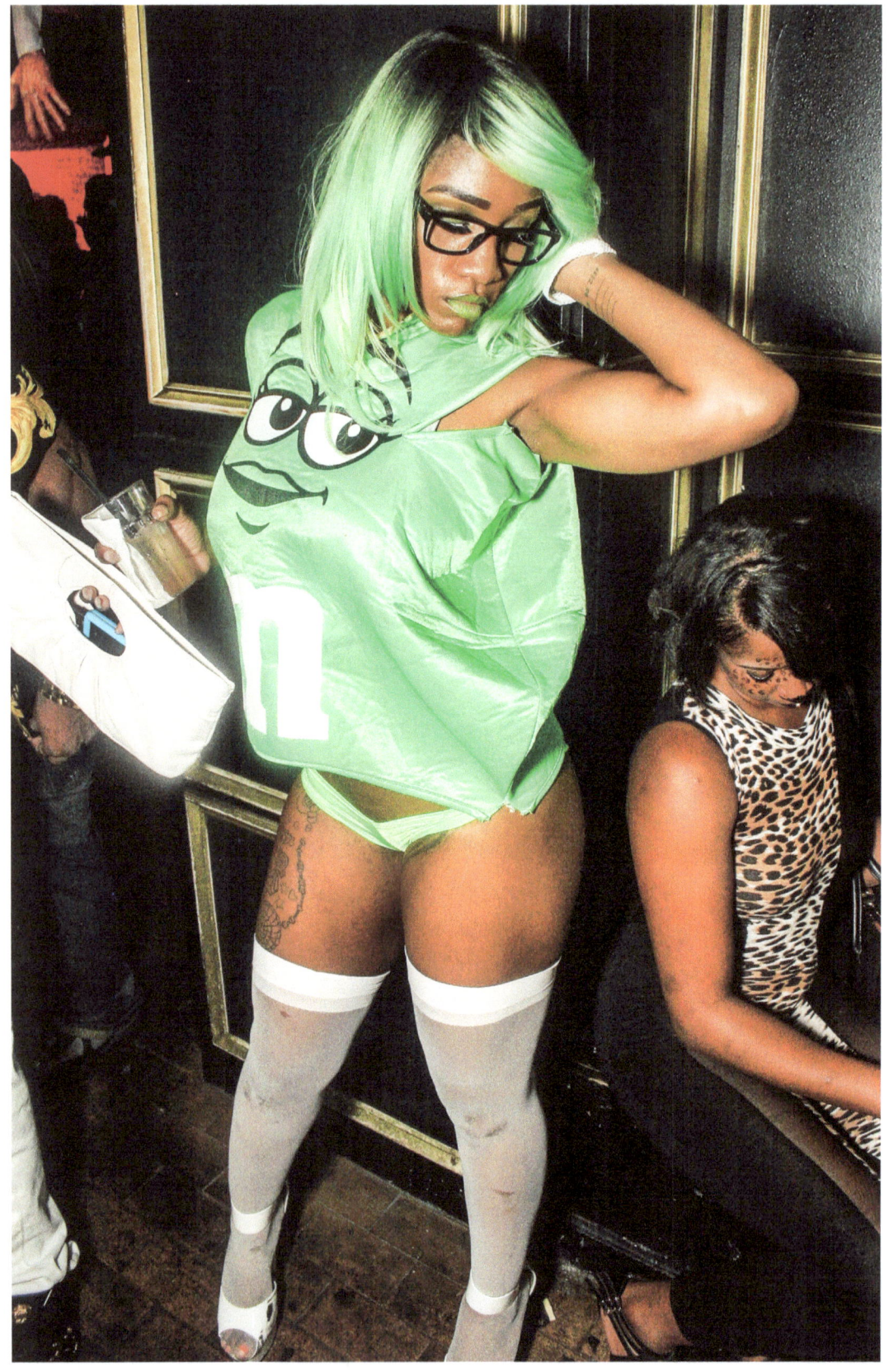

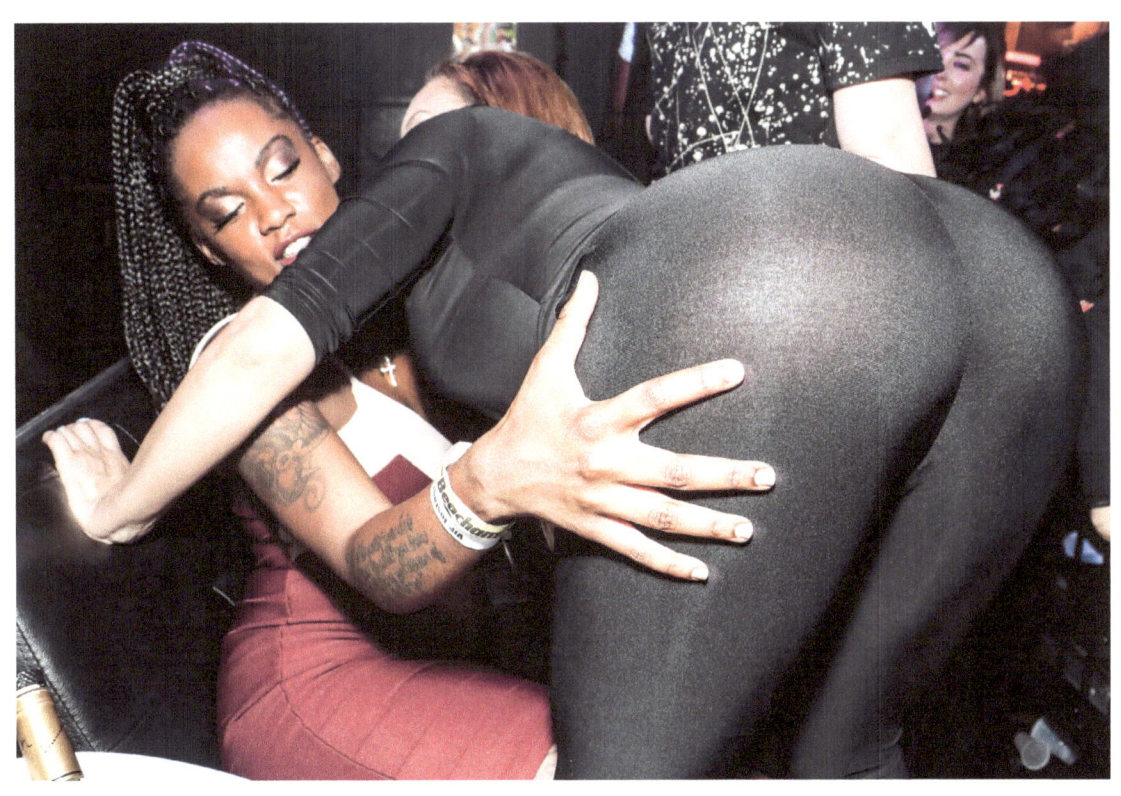
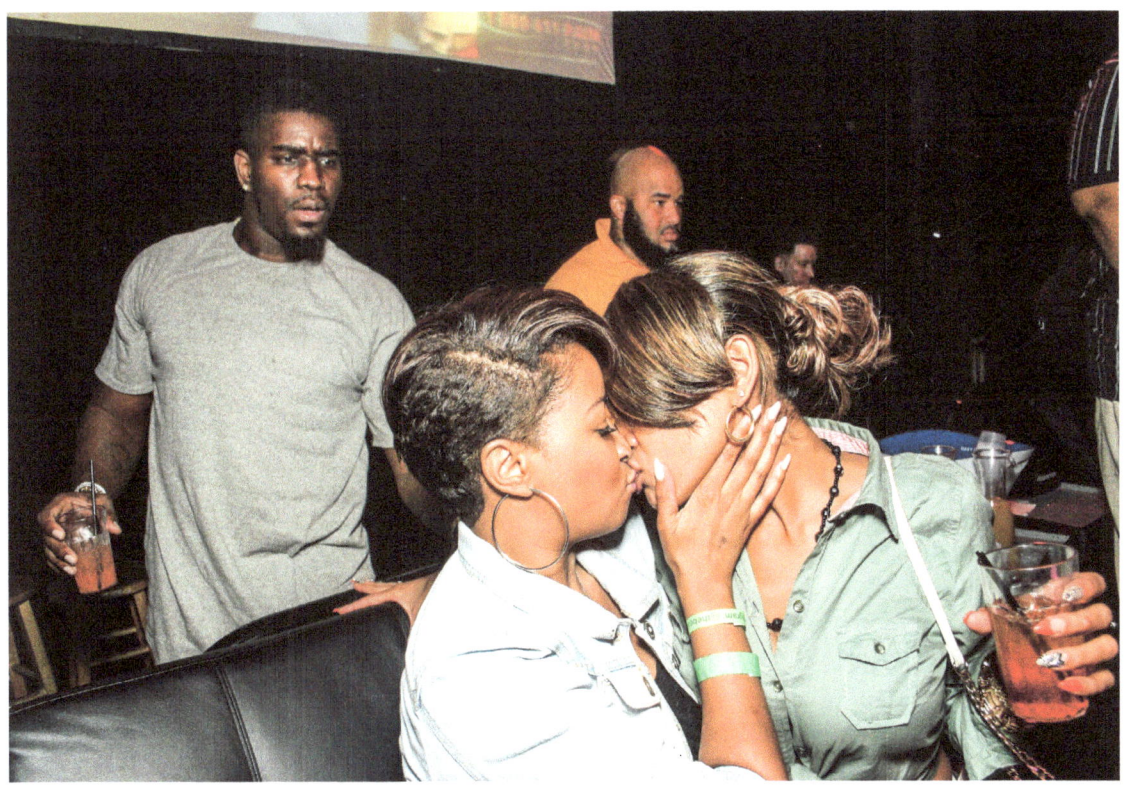

Standing Out

Rather stand out.
Hate trying to be like everyone else.
Too damned boring.
Too damned restrictive.
Too damned time-consuming.
Too damned stupid.

Some folks judge you anyway.
Always finding the cracks in your sidewalk.
Rarely saying anything positive about you.
Always saying something negative.

Hate folks telling me what to believe.
Or what to read.
What to listen to.
What to wear.
What to eat.
What to drink.
How to express myself.
Who to hang around.
Who to marry.
Wish some folks would mind their own goddamned business.

Don't know the rules sometimes.
Try playing them.
Next thing I know?
I played the wrong rules.
Or the rules have changed.
Now, I'm the fool again.
The idiot.
The cave person who should've known better.

Reason why I avoid trying to fit in.
Too damned time-consuming.
Too damned restrictive.
Too damned stupid.

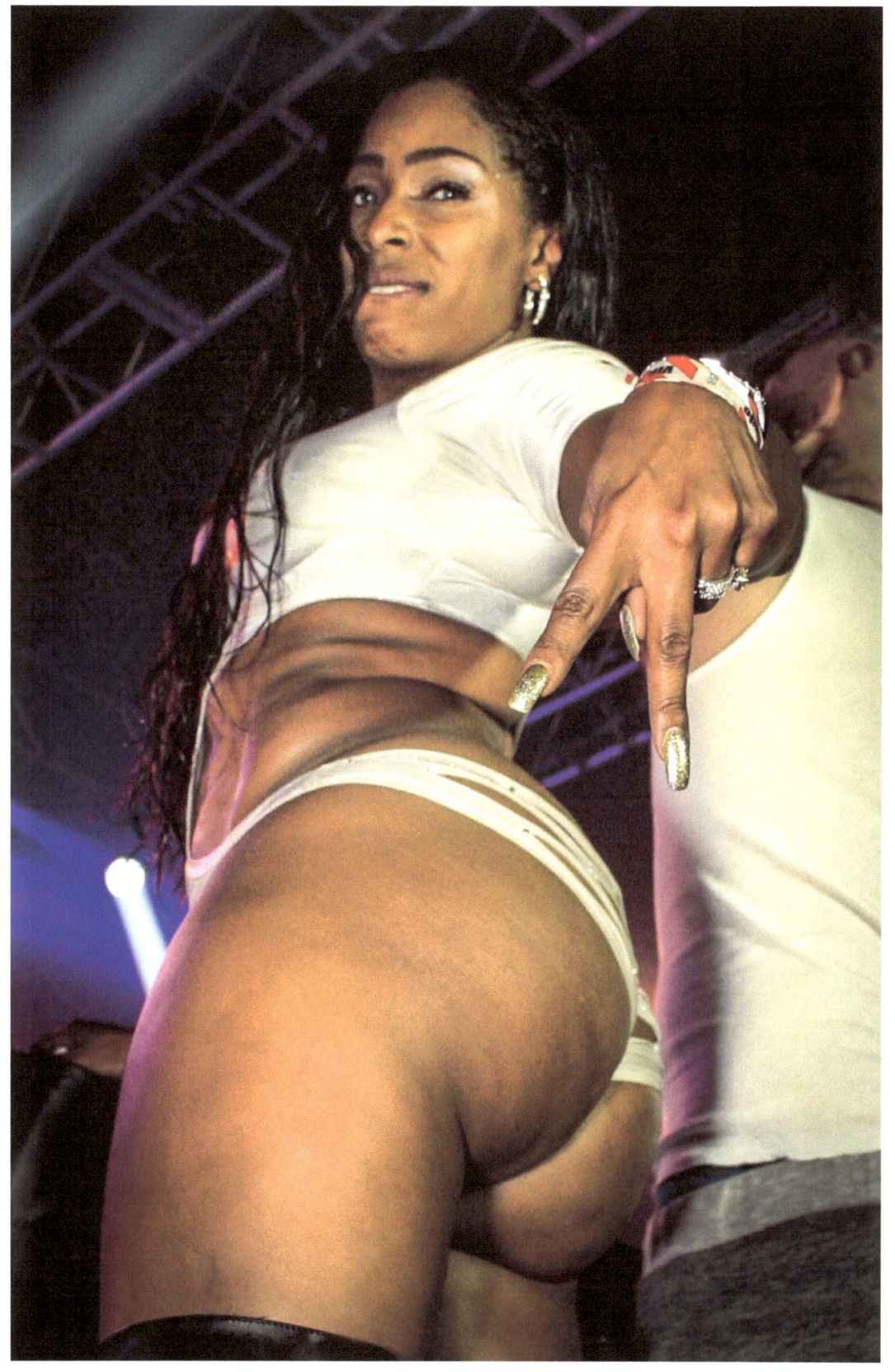

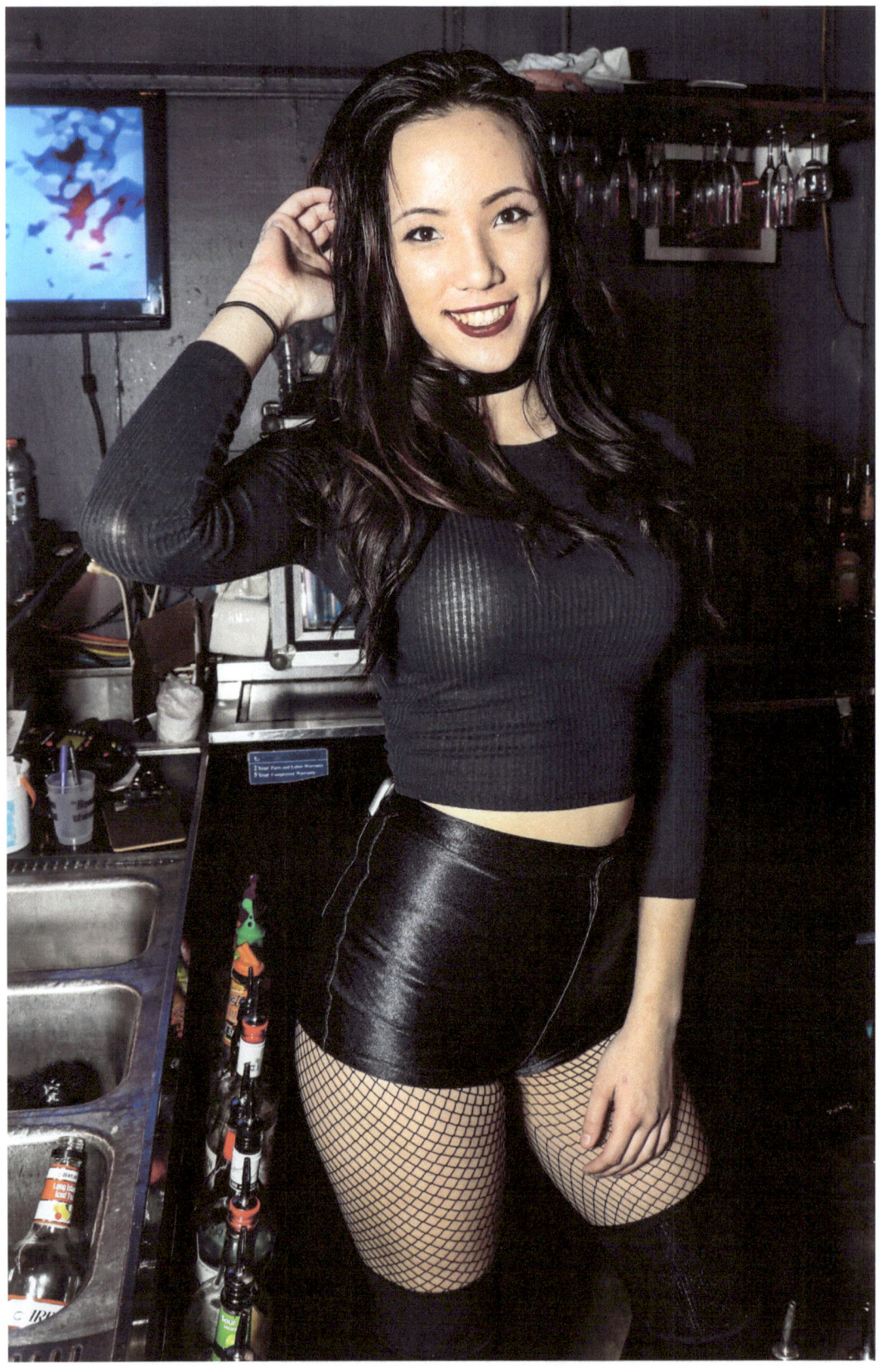

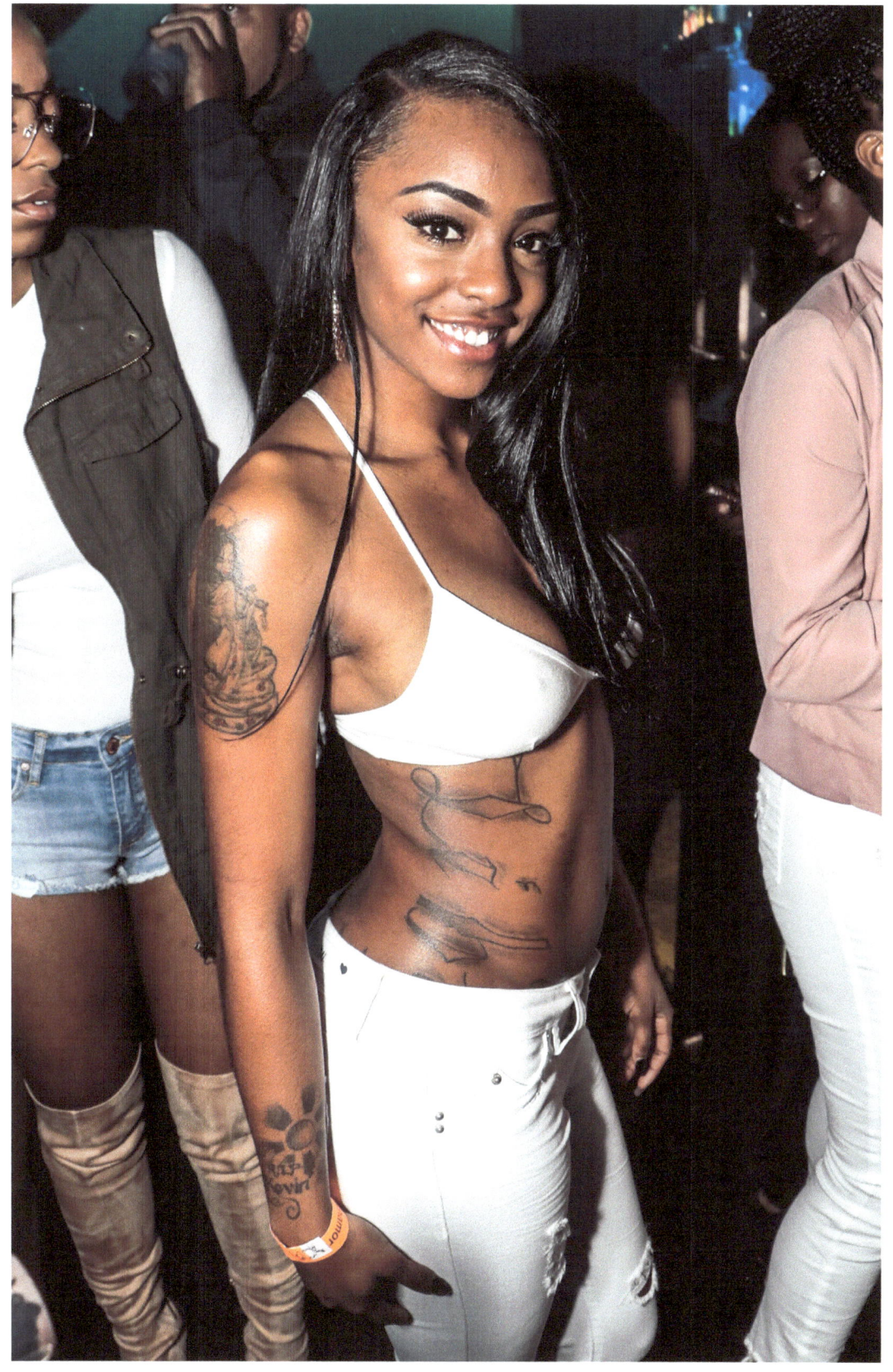

English Teacher

School years.
Heard a nasty rumor about an English teacher.
Rumor said she sexed male students.

Heard the rumor from a kid in shop class.
Kid was telling rumor to everyone sitting at the table.

Rumor was probably just a rumor.
Always remembered dude for running his mouth.

Same teacher liked my poetry.
Wasn't a bad-looking woman.
Had a nice backside.
Nothing happened between us.
Besides, I failed her class.

Present day.
Thinking about her now.
Did I have bragging rights?
Did I have permission to talk some shit?

Lost a school writing contest that year.
Wasn't even given honorable mention.
Yet, English teacher with nice backside liked my poetry.

Folks trash-talking my poetry?
I can always remember her.
English teacher with nice backside who liked my poetry.

Realizing the answer to my question.
Yep, I damned sure did have bragging rights.

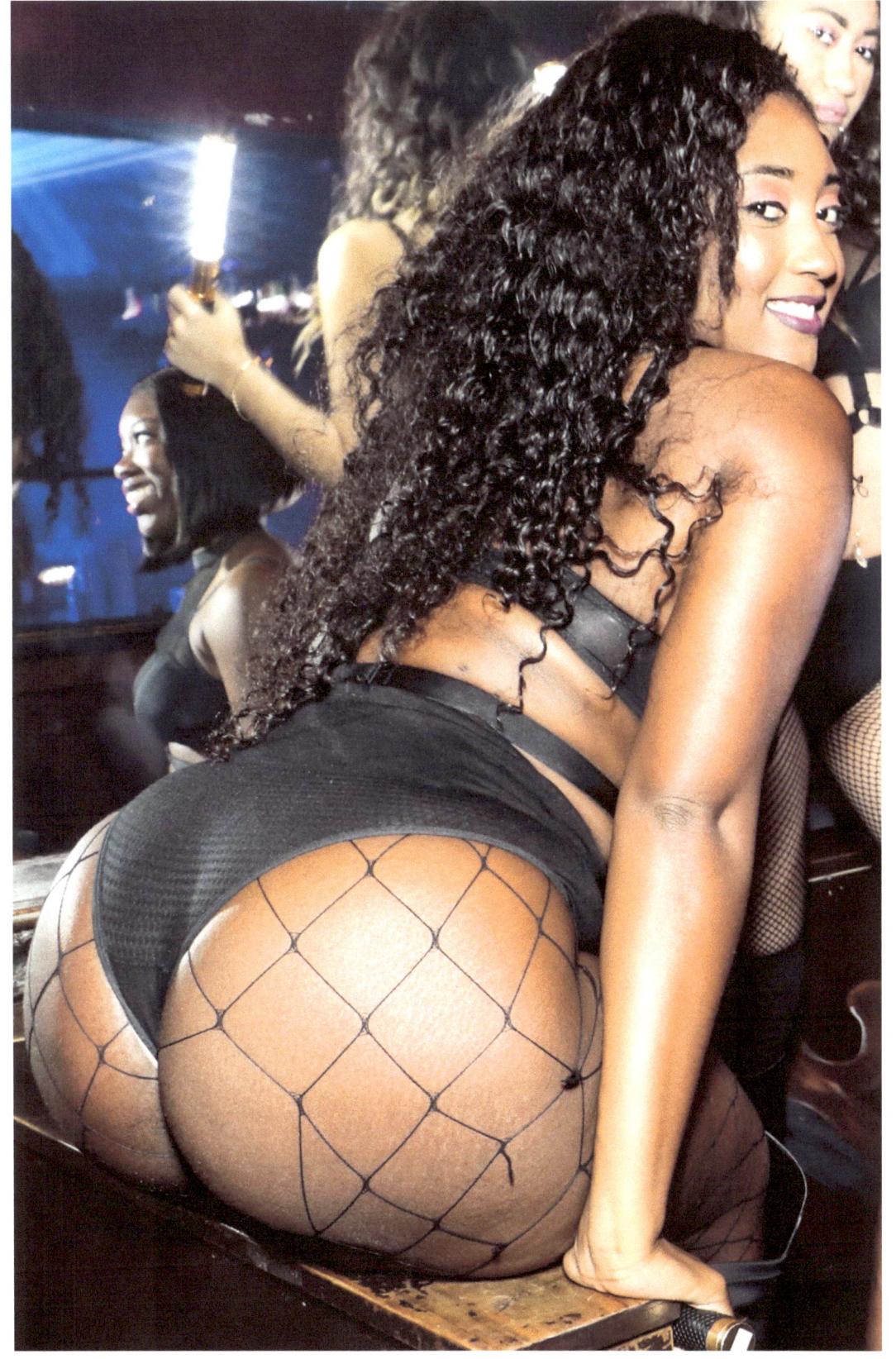

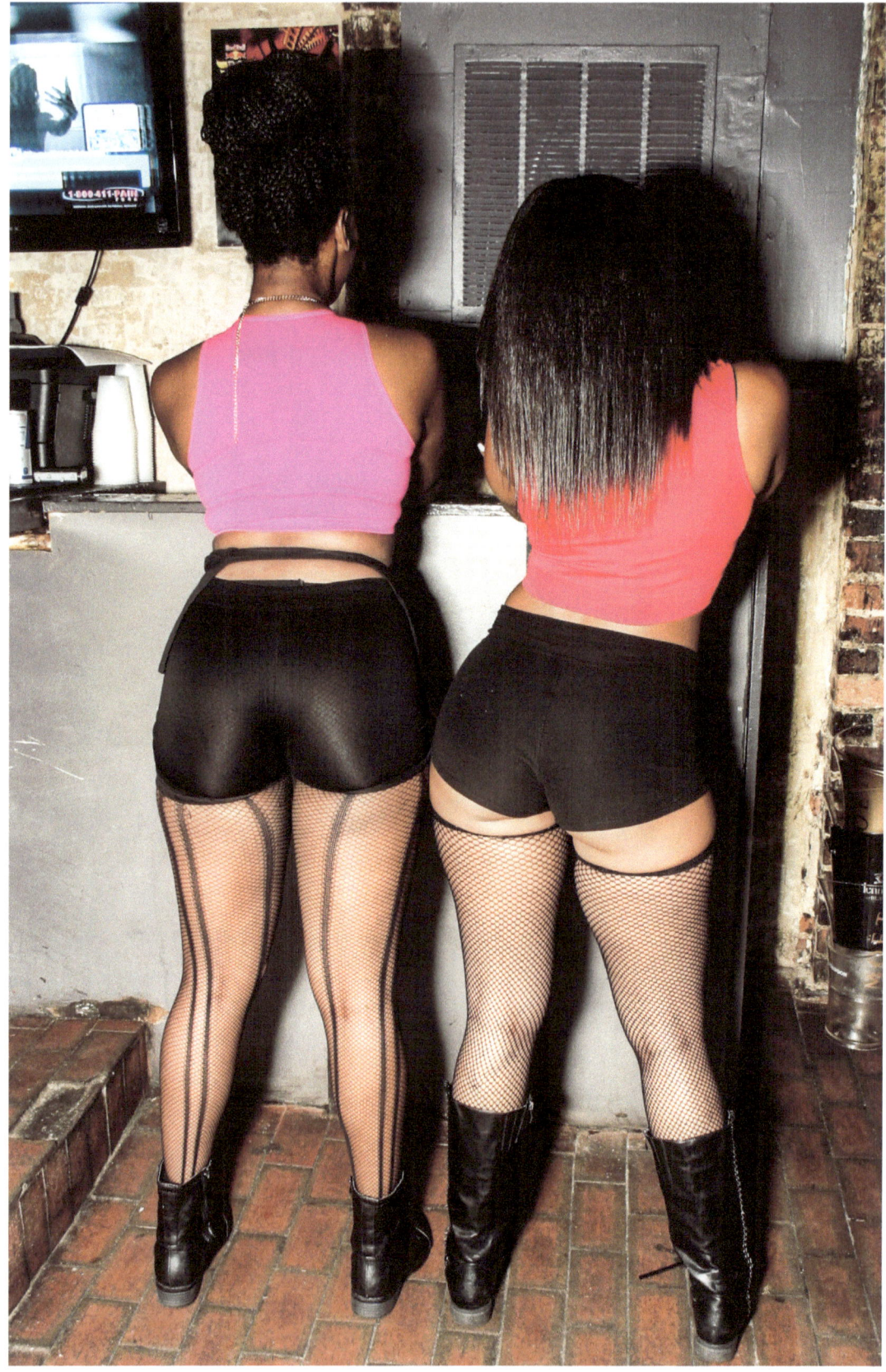

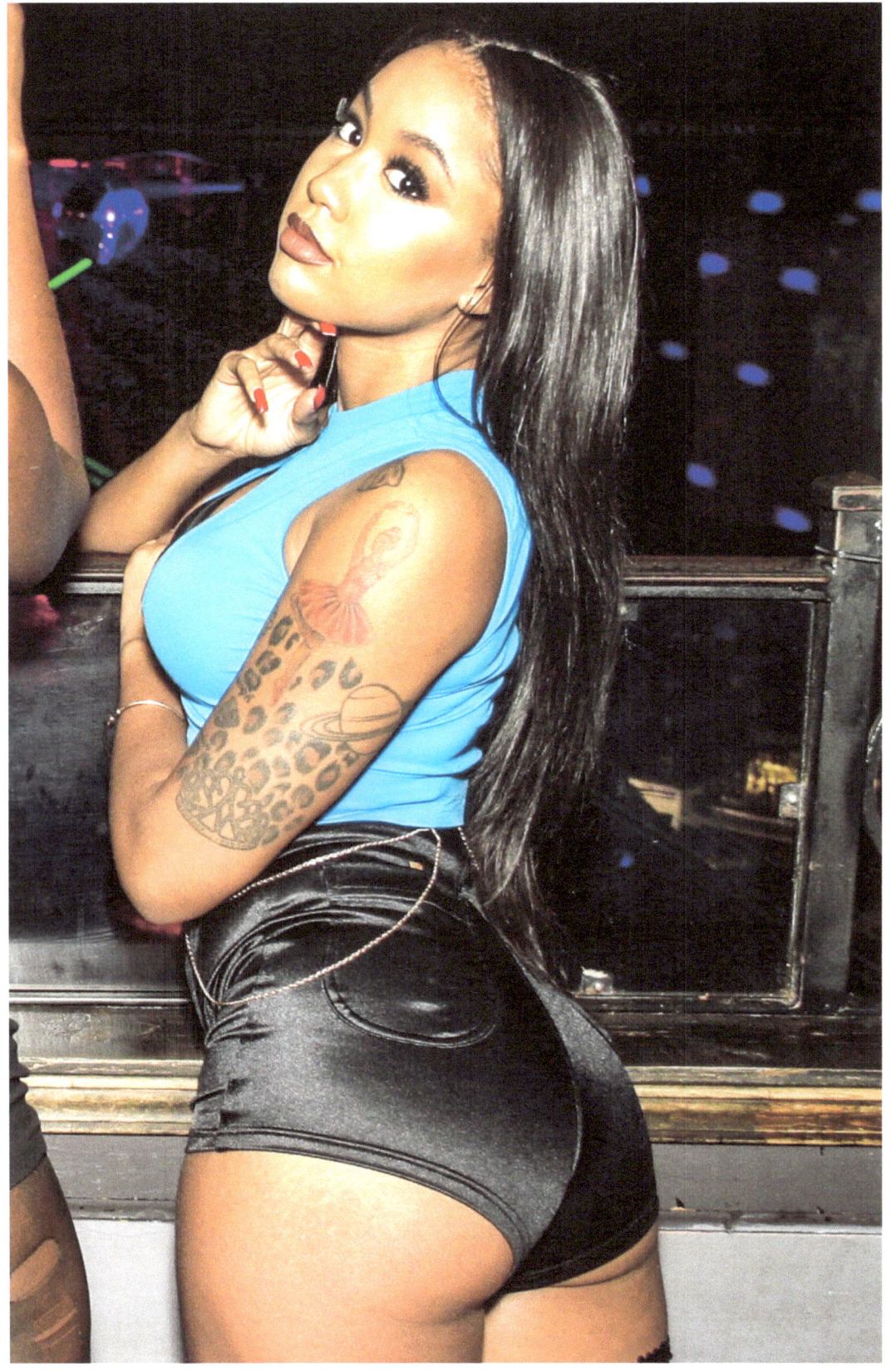

Losing the House

Hated being evicted.
Had to leave favorite stuff behind.
Brother and his family had to adopt my cat.
Still, late mother's house had to go.
Too much money owed to mortgage company.

1998.
Late mother paid down payment on house.
House was seventy-two thousand dollars.

2016.
Later mother died.
Now, one hundred and thirty-nine thousand dollars
owed to mortgage company.
One hundred and thirty-nine thousand dollars
owed on a house that was originally
seventy-two thousand dollars.
Not enough life insurance money to cover that.

I refused to continue payments.
Stayed in house for over two years.
Enjoyed every damned bit of it.
Nobody bothering me.
Television loud as I wanted.
Didn't have to deal with roommates eating up my
food.

Always wanted to live alone.
Just couldn't afford it.
Now, wish came true.

Had a lawyer representing me during foreclosure.
Paid him three-fifty a month.
Yet, knew I had to eventually leave house.

Was worried I couldn't find a place to live.
Yet, I did.

Glad late mother's house is behind me now.
Hated being evicted.
Still, too much money owed to mortgage company.
Late mother's house had to go.

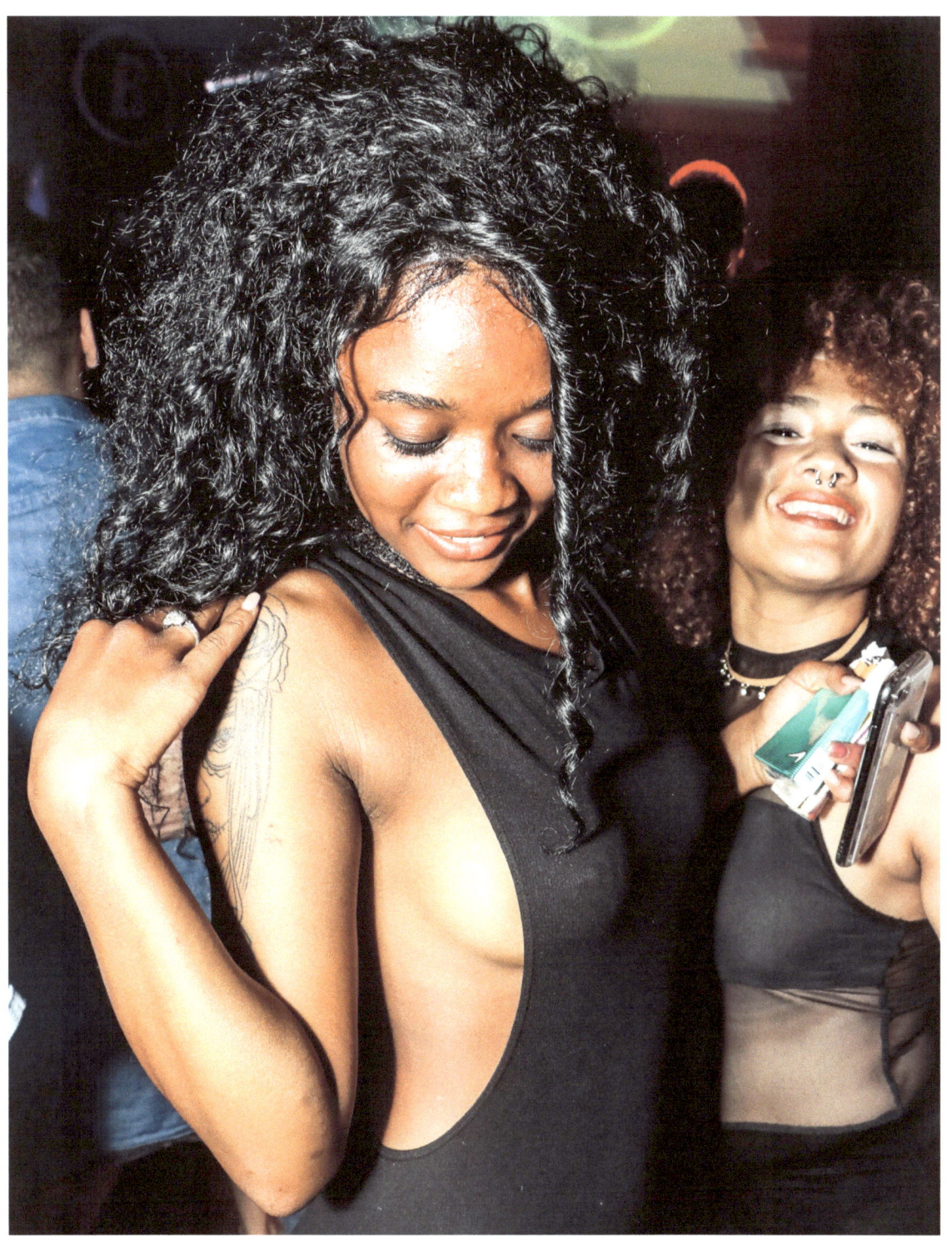

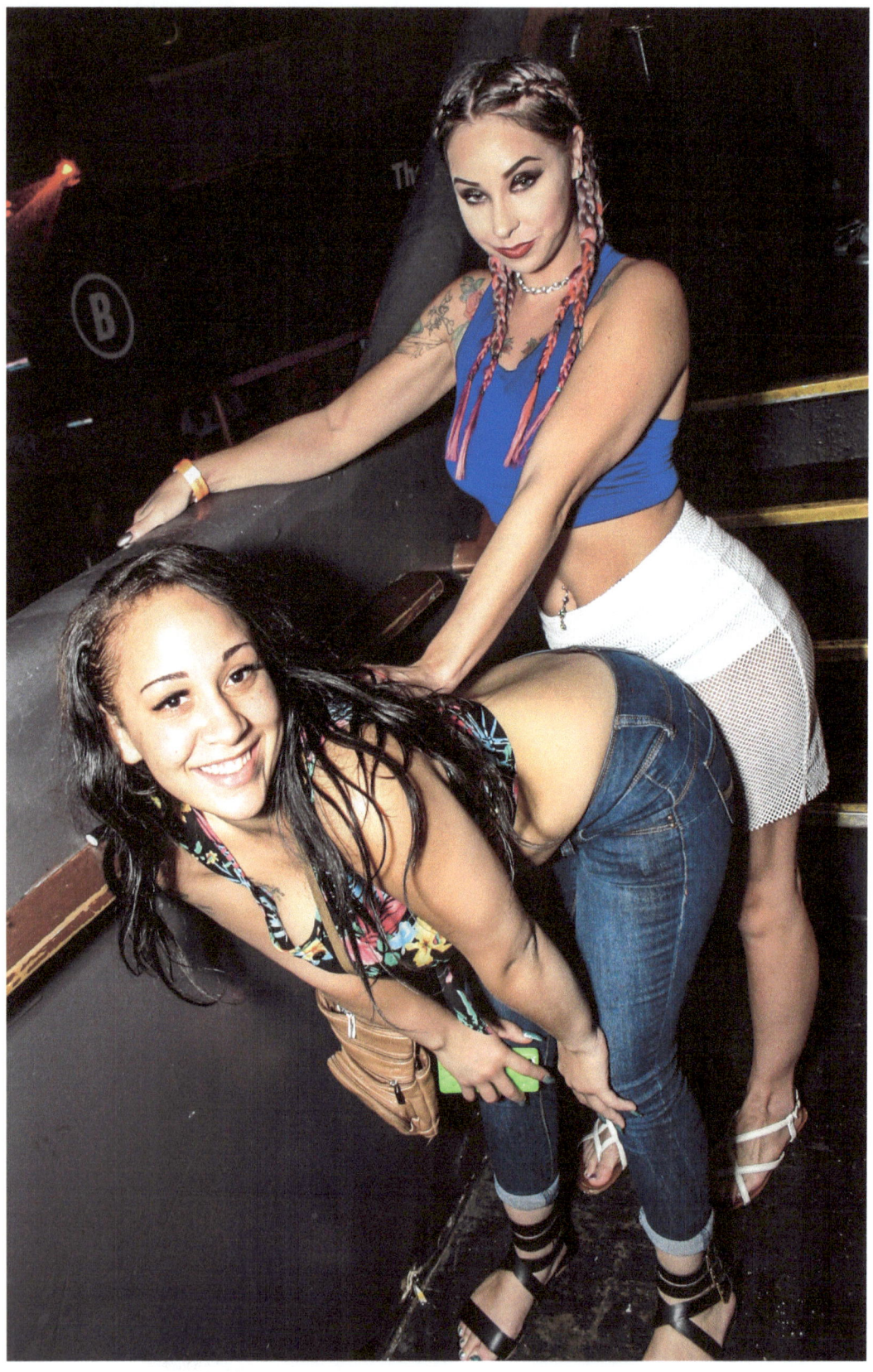

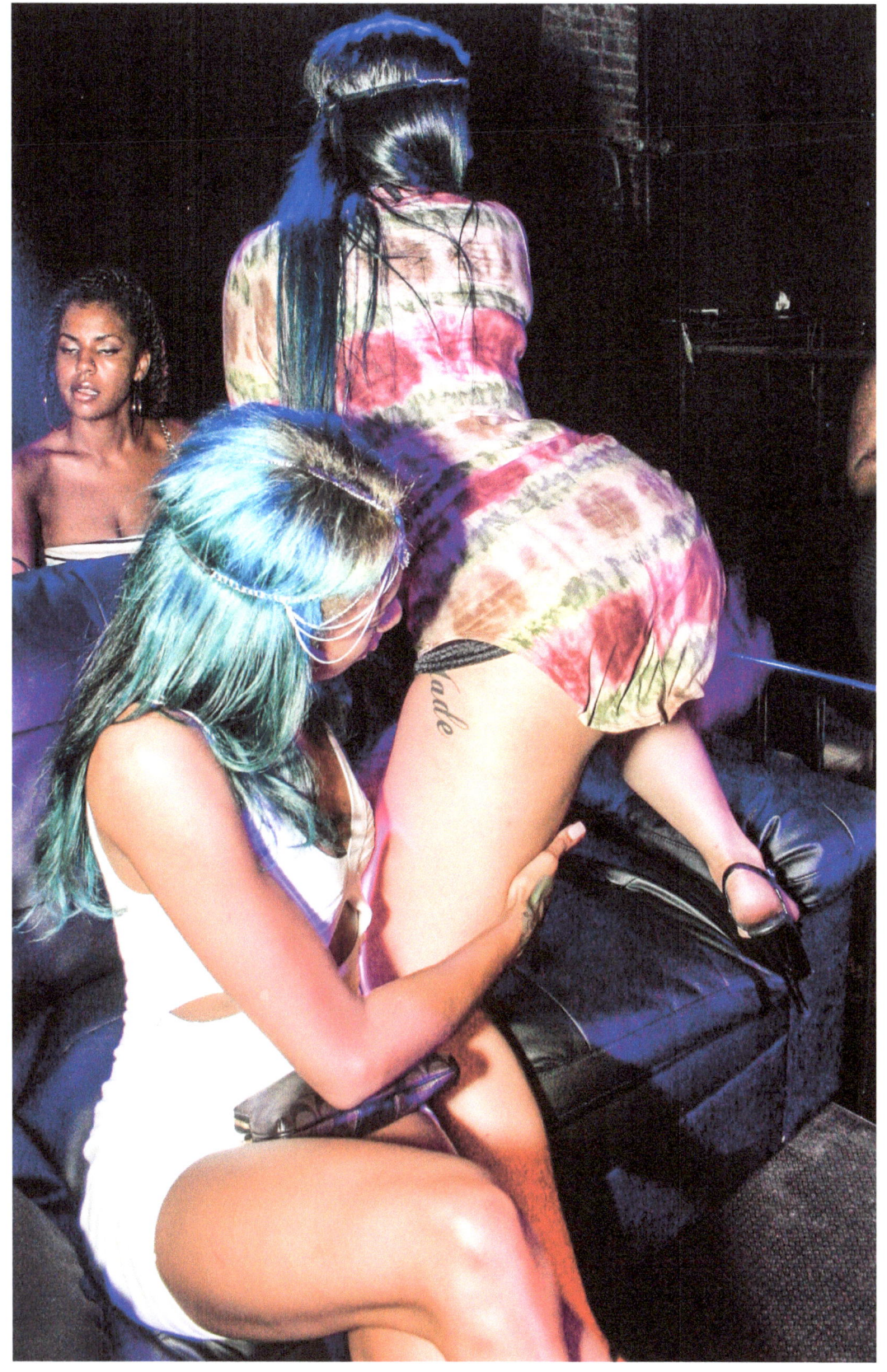

Judging Women

Who am I to judge women's bodies?
Have imperfections of my own.
Won't be walking around shirtless anytime soon.

Many dudes in same situation.
But quick to judge women.
Fat dudes.
Ugly dudes.
Always have something to say.

Fat dudes always badmouthing big women.
Never could understand that.
Shouldn't fat dudes be paying attention to their own waistlines?

Ugly dudes always calling women ugly.
Remember one ugly dude calling women in my photos monsters.
Can hear some women talking about him now.

"I know he ain't talking about somebody."

Have my own guilt in foolishness.
Made jokes about a politician's wife.
Kept talking about her lacking in the booty department.

Should be ashamed of myself.
Who am I to go around talking about people?

Have imperfections of my own.

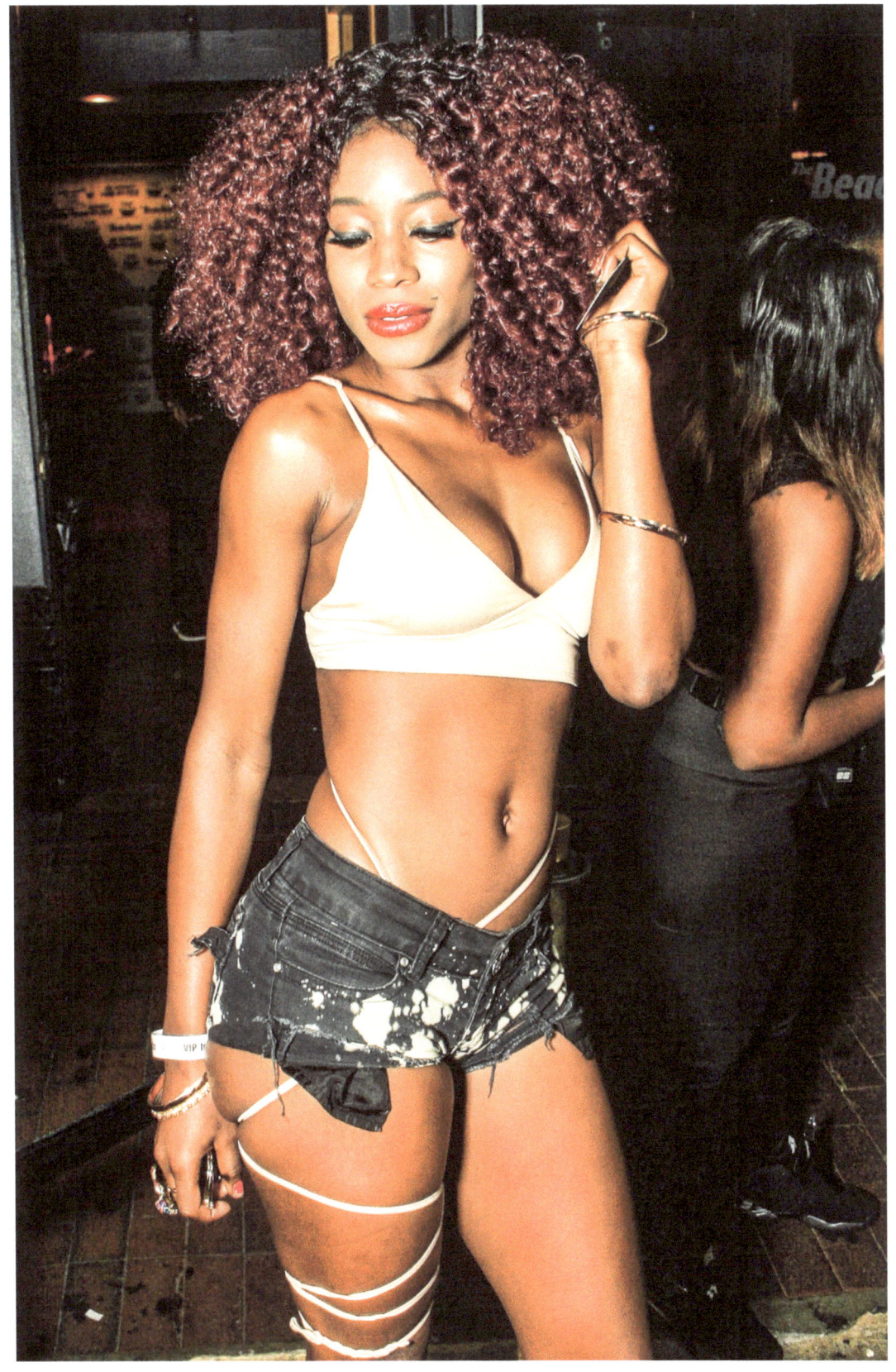

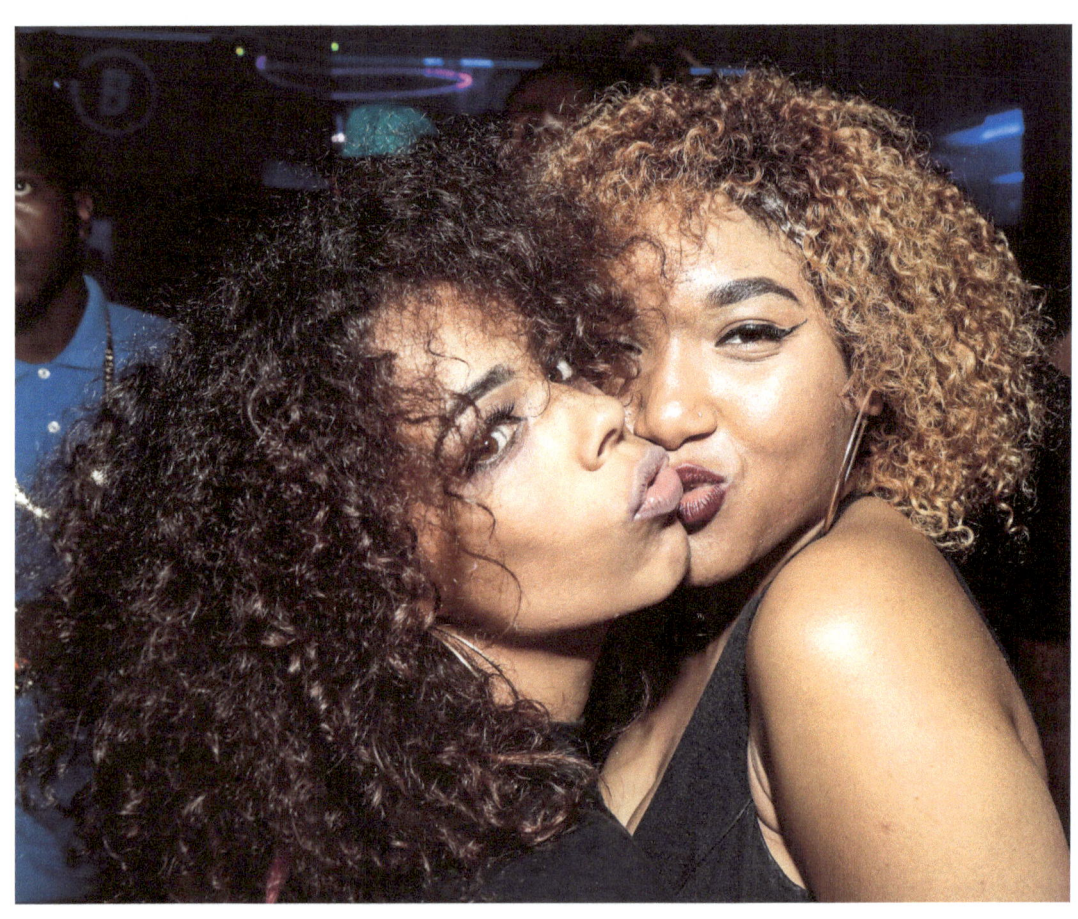

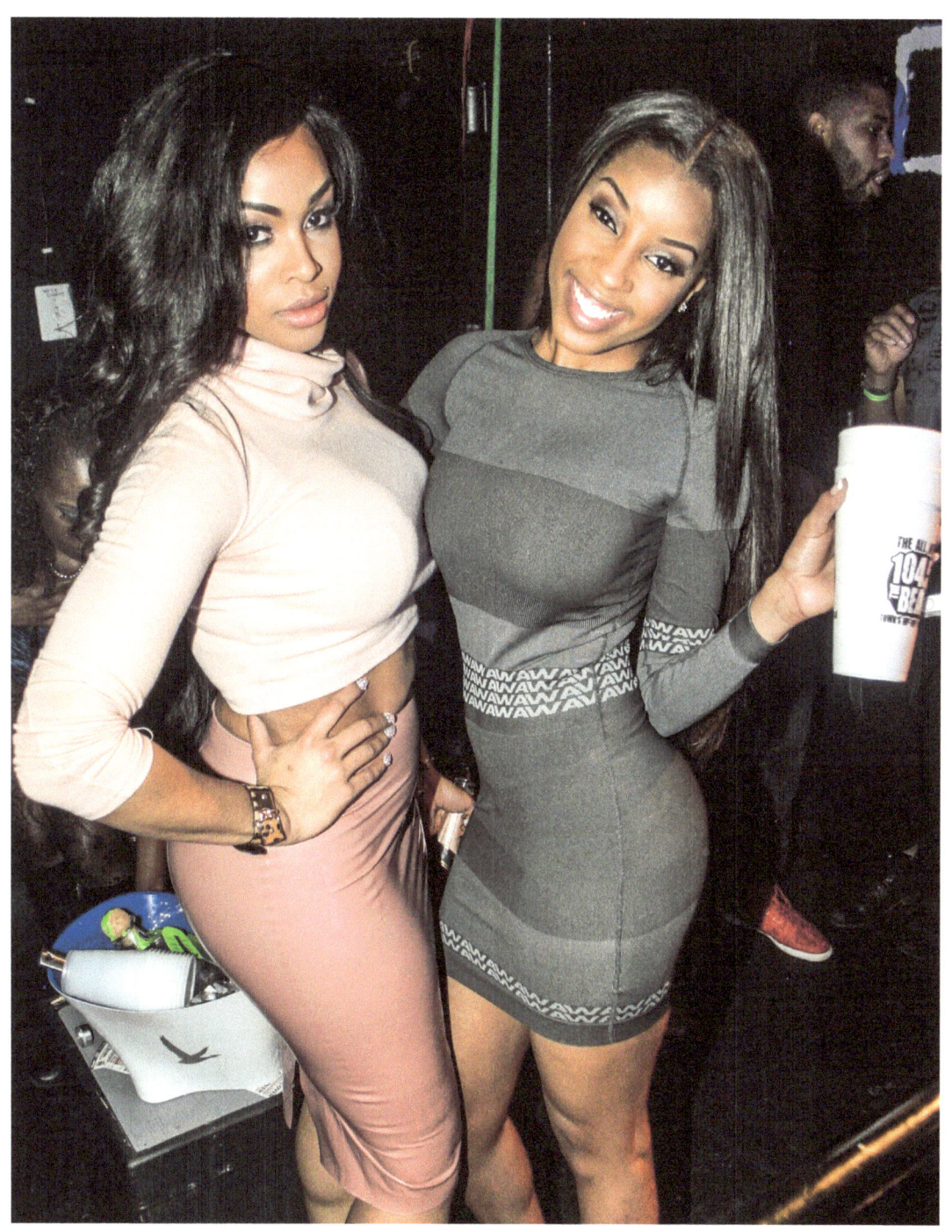

Nocturnal Creature

Nocturnal.
Definition?
People who are active at night.
A word I learned recently about myself.

Studies describe nocturnal people as smart and creative.
(Well, I'll get back to you on that one.)
Studies say nocturnal people lag in academics.
(Nope, I didn't finish college.)
Studies say nocturnal people eat unhealthily.
(Uh huh, that explains my high blood pressure.)

Use to think being nocturnal was a hindrance.
A pain in the ass.
Hated not being able to sleep at night.
Many times, I still can't sleep at night.

Now, I embrace being nocturnal.

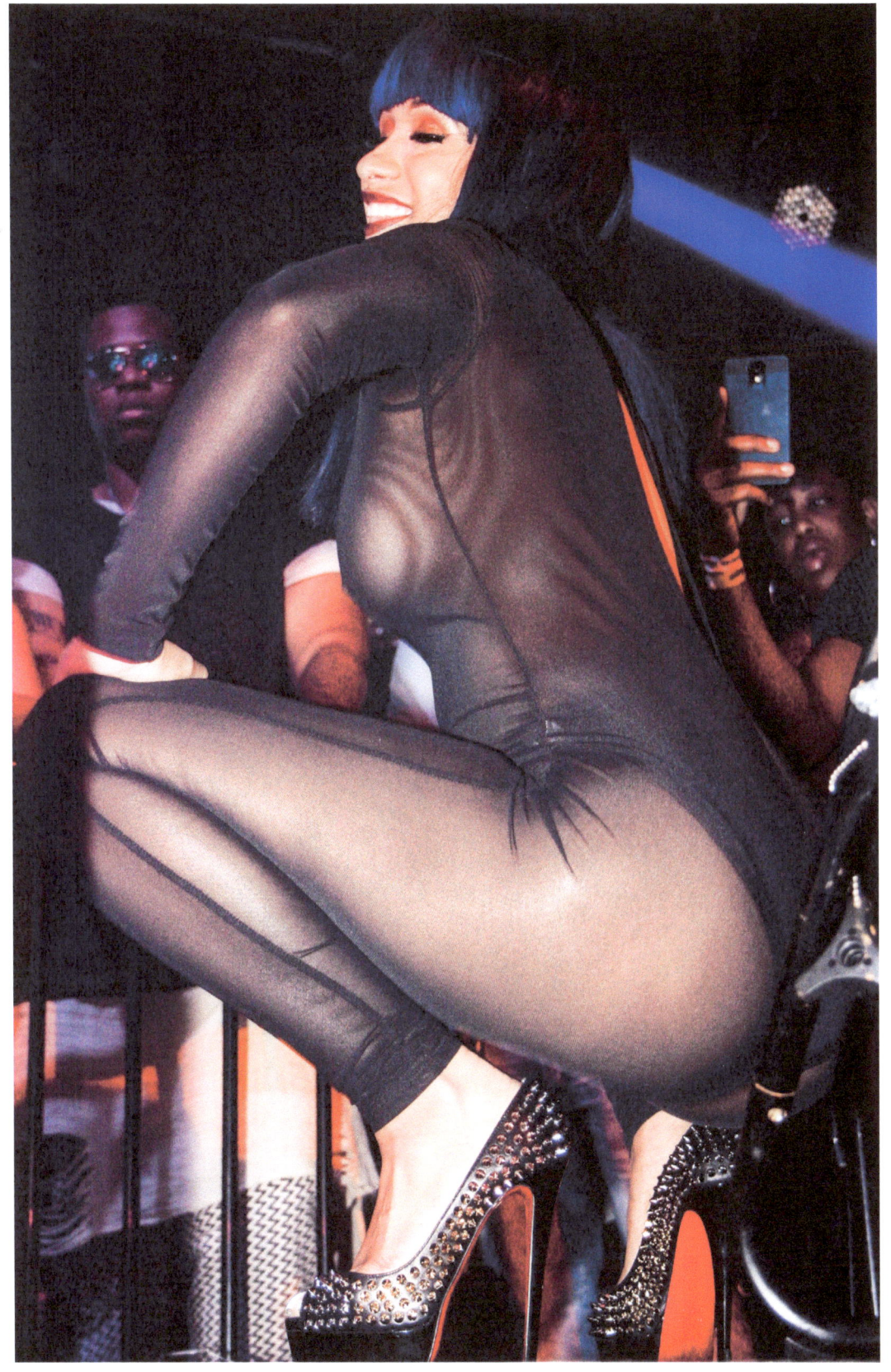

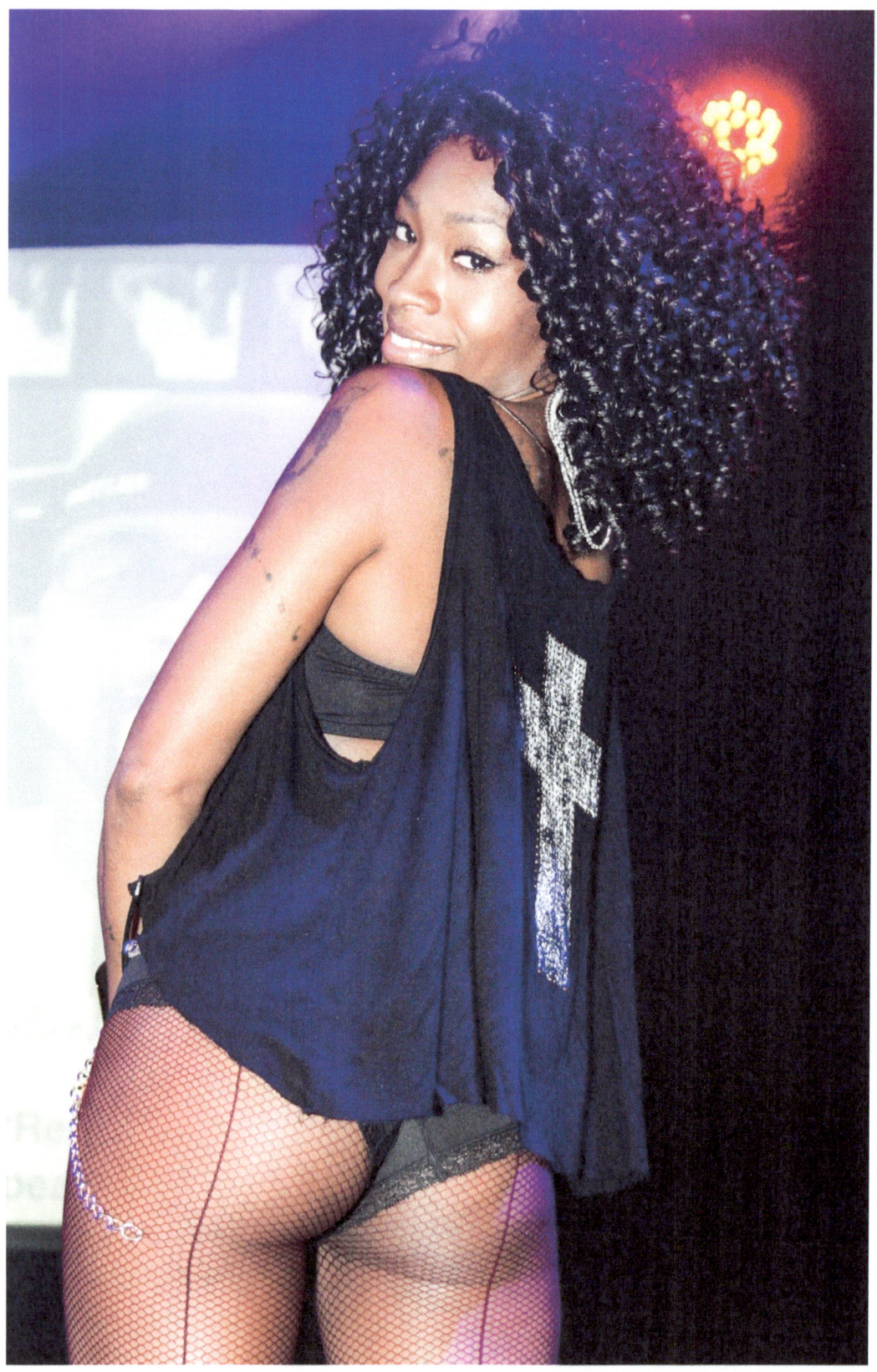

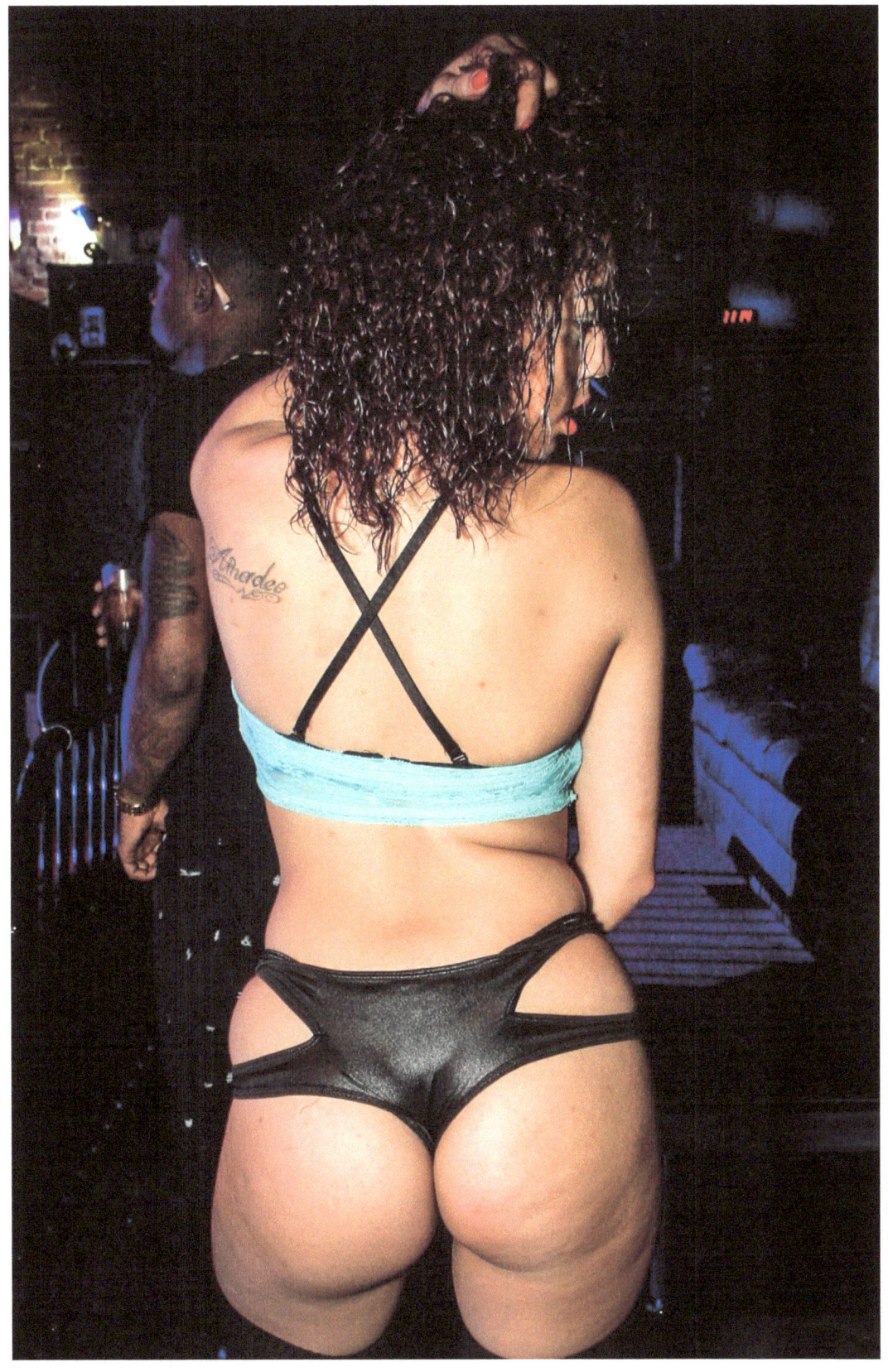

Fighting Love Addiction

Avoided her social media for a whole year.
Used to look at it all the time.
Had to break my addiction to her.
Cyberstalking wasn't helping.

Typed the goal down in my journal.

Avoid her social media for a whole year.

First, I blocked her.
Not just on social media.
Also, on my mobile phone.

Another thing.
Avoided places I knew she patronized.
Plus watched YouTube videos about narcissists.

Took a while.
Almost took ten months.
Yet, avoiding her social media worked.
Showed me the possible true person.
The one she tried to hide.

Remembering what she said about her husband.
Said dude refused having sex with her.
Now realizing she was probably lying.
Creating an excuse to cheat behind his back.

Remembering her saying she was divorcing him.
Probably another lie.
Saying anything to keep me around.
Yet, always came up with excuses.
Excuses on why a divorce never happened.

Had to break up with her.
Always felt uneasy.
Felt her saying she loved me came along too soon.
Barely knew me.
Yet, claimed she loved me.
Said she believed we were soul mates.

Something just didn't seem right about her.

Always wondered about the guy who dated her before me.
Why date a married woman for nearly eight months?
What the hell was he expecting?

Now, I think I know the answer.
Woman probably told him the same things she told me.
Told him she was in love.
Told him she was leaving her husband.
Probably used that soul mates line too.
Probably said anything to keep him around.

Realizing my own fault in this.
Should've ran when she said she was married.

Guess loneliness kept me around.
Too desperate for romance probably did too.
Regardless, I hold responsibility for my own actions.

Damned glad I avoided her social media for a whole year.
It broke my addiction to a married woman.

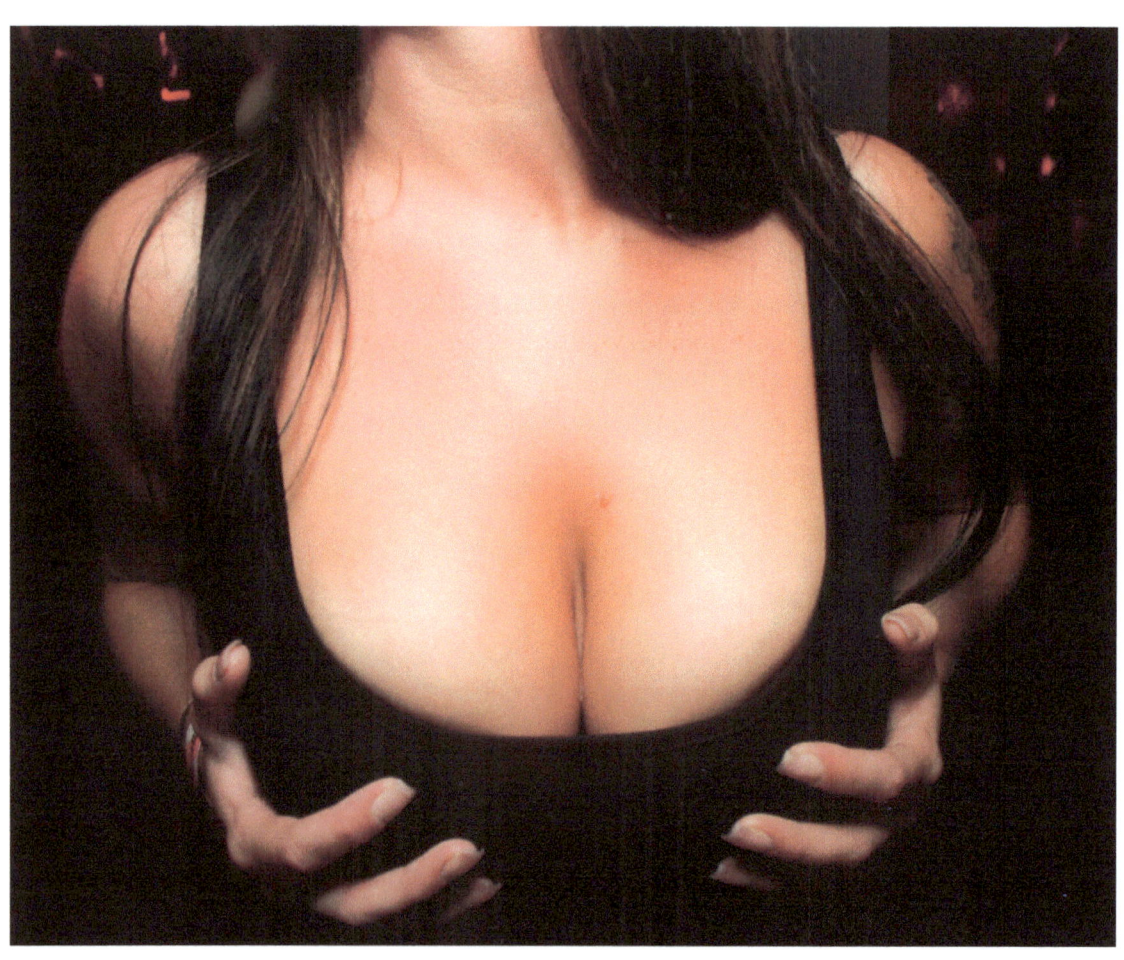

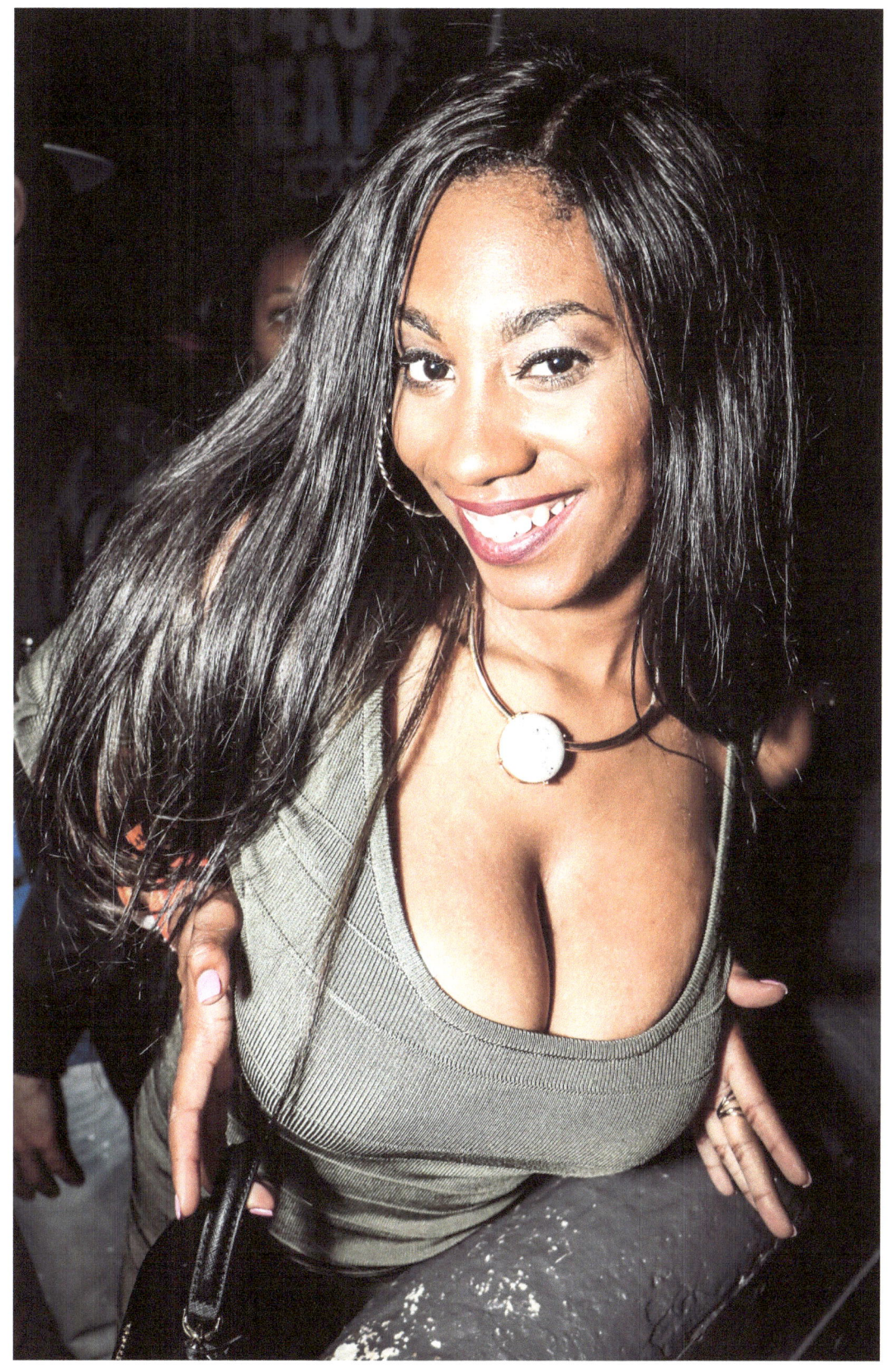

Take It Down, Please

Requests come occasionally.
Some aren't requests at all.
More like demands.
Women make these requests more than dudes.
Requests for me to remove pictures of them from social media.

One woman claimed she worked for an important law firm.
Pool party pic wasn't a good look for her company.

One person claimed some pics made him look crazy.
(By the way, that same dude wound up committing suicide years later.)

One woman claimed ex-husband was going to take her kids.
My pics of her partying would be the blame.

Another woman claimed she had a stalker.
Another one claimed the same thing.

One woman complained about my booty pic of her and her friend.
Loved that pic.
Them was some good-looking booties.
Yet, woman claimed booty pic wasn't a good look for her business.

I usually take the pics down.
Pain in the ass.
But I do it anyway.

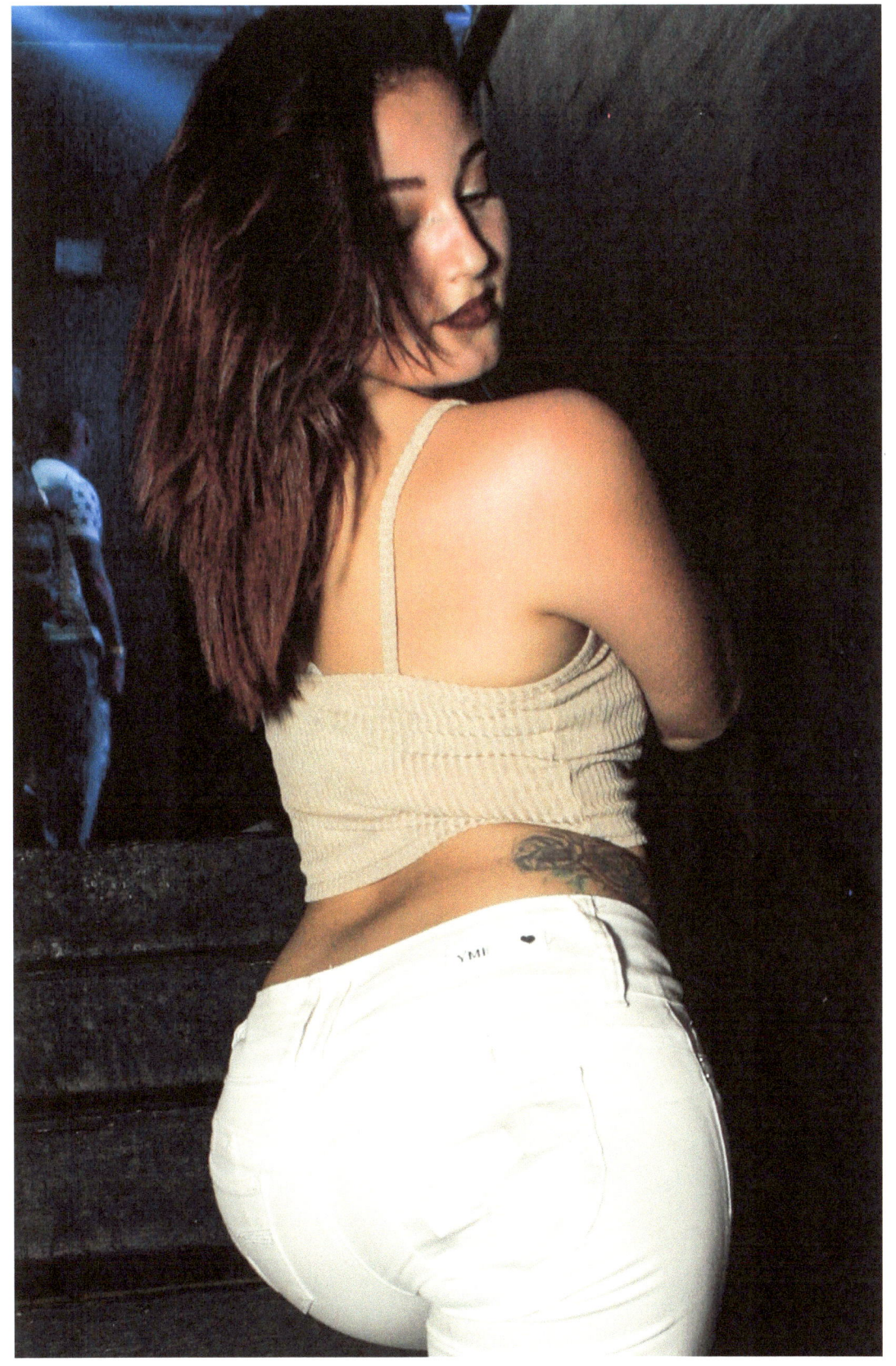

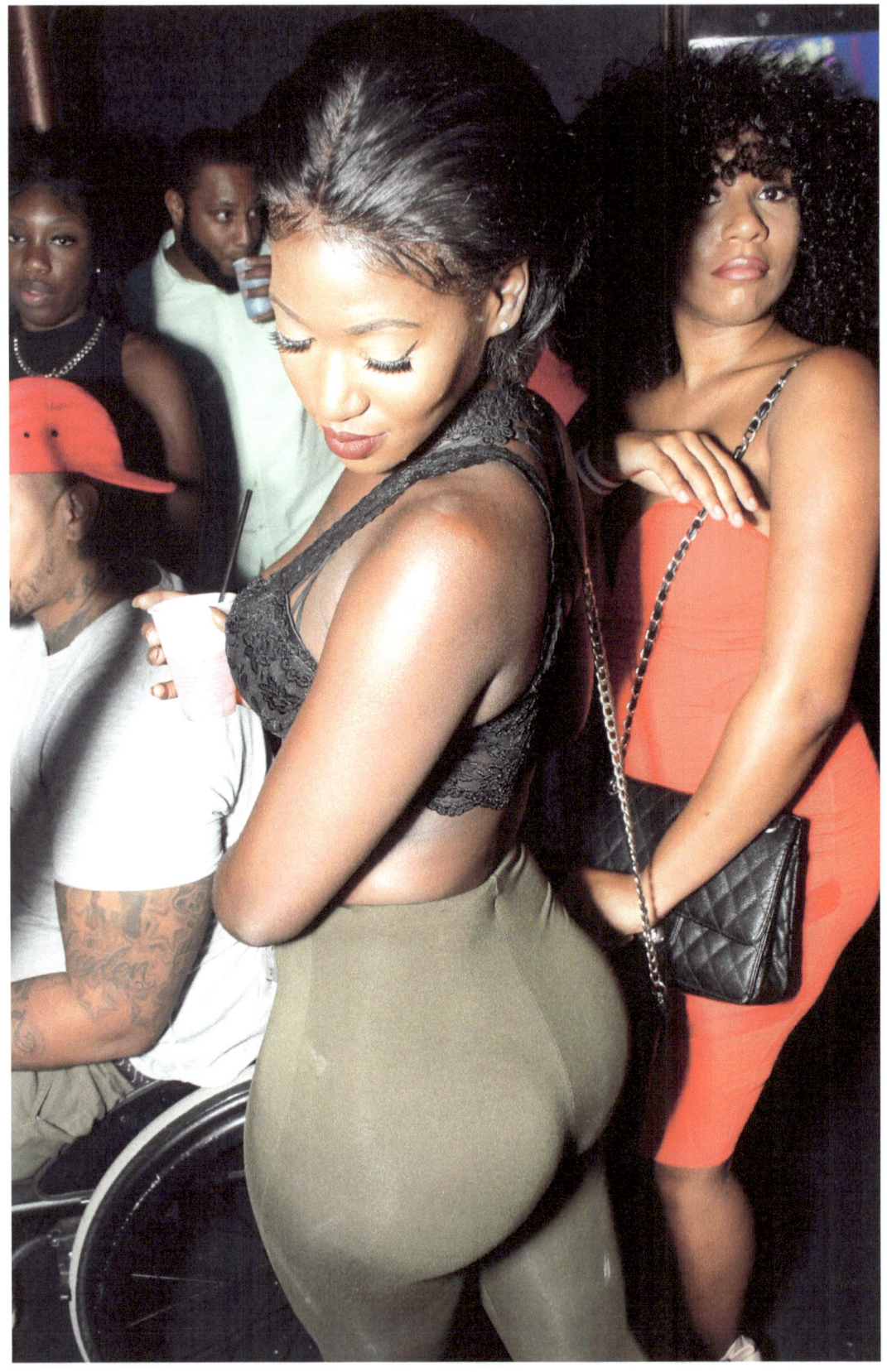

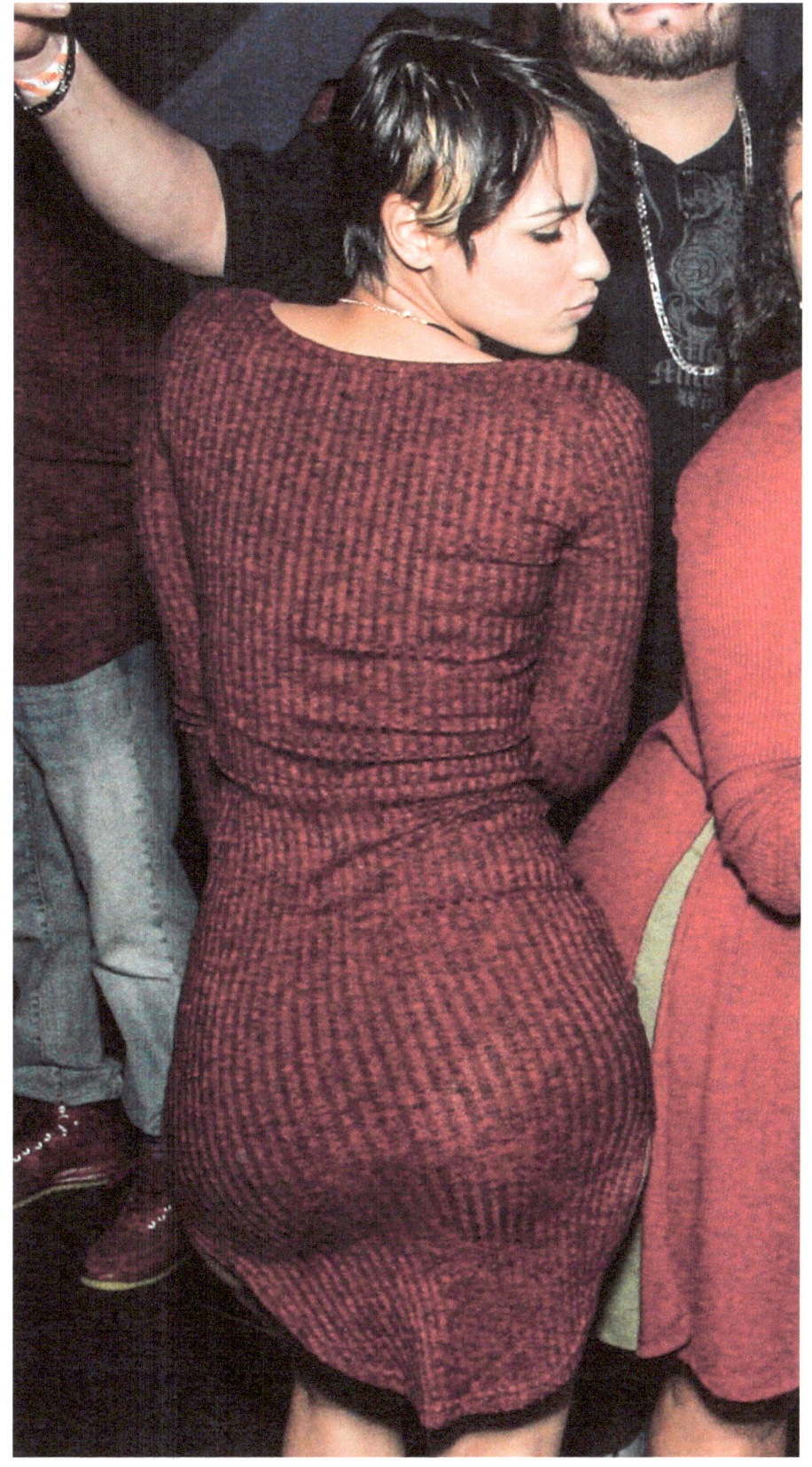

An Adult Child's Mixed Emotions

Thinking about my late mother.
Bad memories.
Good memories.

Verbally abused me.
Always aimed spirit-breaking words at me.

Yet, encouraged me to keep writing.

Didn't want me speaking to my biological father.
Nor speak to my other brothers and sisters he fathered.

Yet, gave my stepfather hell when he messed with me.
Least most of the time she did.

Always thought she favored my younger brother over me.
Seemed to always praise him more than she did me.

Yet, held a secret no one knew about.
Made me the primary beneficiary of her life insurance policy.

Sometimes I don't miss her.
The verbal abuse.
The manipulation.
Years of her denying she abused me.
Took that denial to her grave.

Sometimes, I do miss her.
Her and I going to the movies.
Her and I visiting the winery.
Her and I liking Slick Rick.
Can hear her now.

"Knock'em out the box, Rick."

Mixed emotions.
Hard for me to move on.

Still, I try.

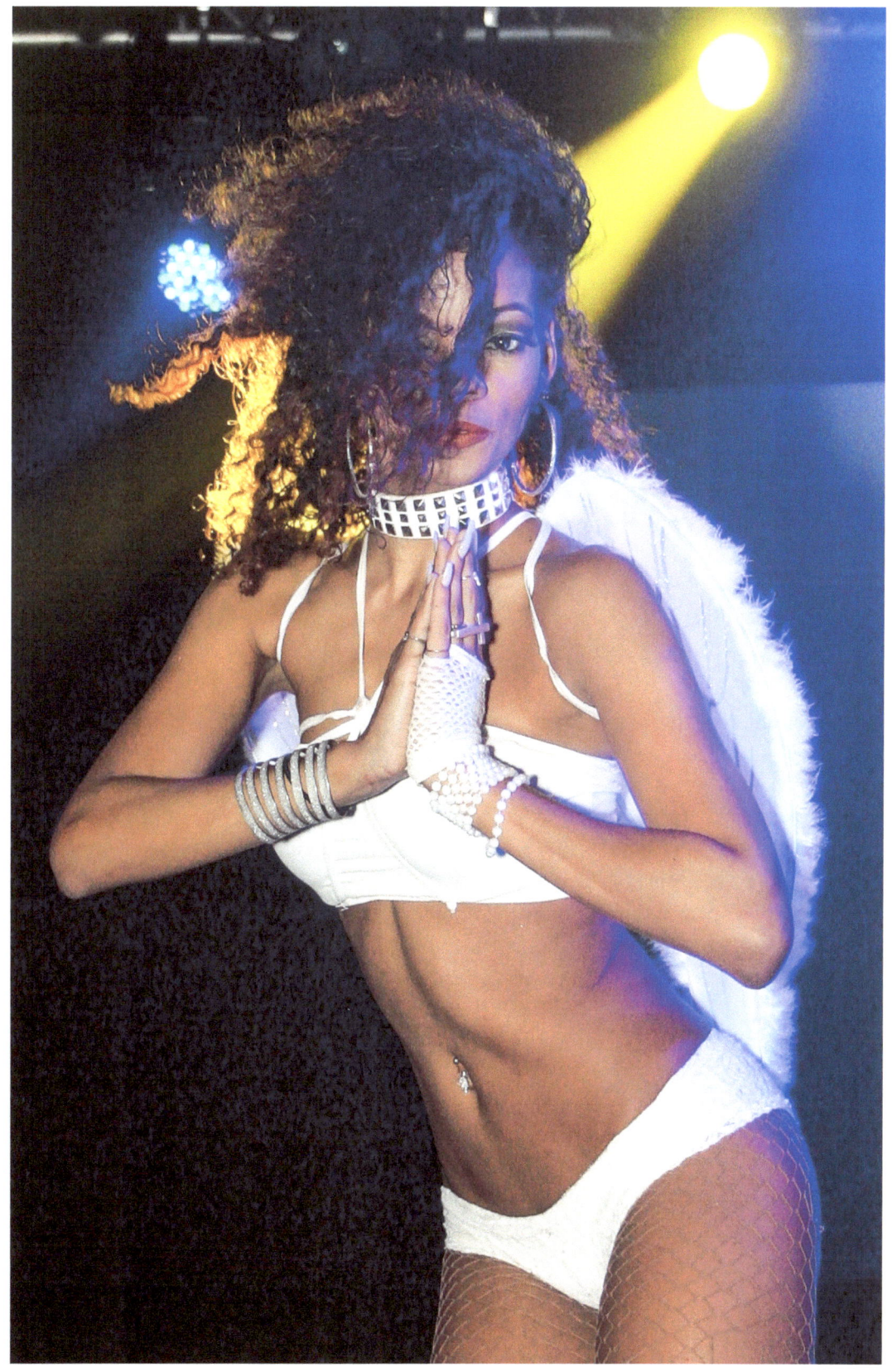

About the Author

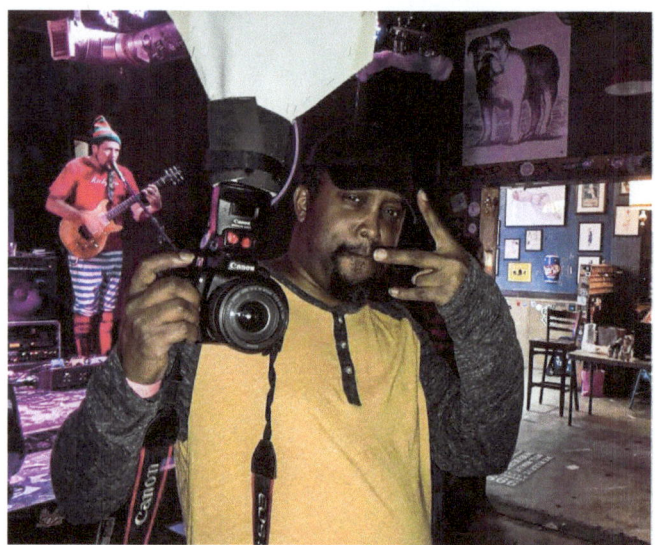

Photo by Jeffro Rapp

Patrick Scott Barnes is a native of Sanford, Florida. *Nightclub Womenz* is his second photo and poetry book. His first such book was *Three Orlando Nightspots*.

For nearly two decades, Barnes has photographed Orlando's nightlife.

Also, he has photographed for alternative publication *Orlando Weekly*.

Most Central Floridians know Patrick Scott Barnes as a poet. For seven years, he hosted Backroom Words, a weekly open-mic poetry reading.

He also opened for the following people: Author and scriptwriter Jerry Stahl, the legendary Lydia Lunch (twice) and poet Beau Sia from the movies *SlamNation* and *Slam*.

Through the now closed CreateSpace, Barnes published two other books: *The Butt Freak Blues* (a book of poetry) and *Photos from the Cell Phone*.

Recently, Patrick Scott Barnes relocated from Orlando back to Sanford.

www.ingramcontent.com/pod-product-compliance
Lightning Source LLC
Chambersburg PA
CBHW051219220526
45473CB00003B/1100